D0710419

SITES

SITES

A THIRD MEMOIR

WALLACE FOWLIE

Duke University Press   Durham 1987

Parts of two chapters in this book have appeared in
The Southern Review and *The Sewanee Review*.
© 1987 Duke University Press
All rights reserved
Printed in the United States of America on
acid-free paper ∞
Library of Congress Cataloging-in-Publication Data
appear on the last printed page of this book.

To Catherine and Thomas Foster

Contents

Introduction: On Writing Autobiography

This kind of writing: a journal or memoirs or simply autobiography, has pre-occupied me now for five or six years. A first volume, *Journal of Rehearsals*, came out in 1978. It was largely concerned with my relationship with France: my early study of French, my first visit to Paris when I was nineteen, and then a few later visits for work on a doctoral dissertation I was trying to write. If there is any coherence in that book, it is the role of France in the life of an American French teacher.

When I received the first copies of that book, I sent one to a good friend and mentor who had been my chairman at Yale at the beginning of my career. He wrote a letter of approval and encouragement. In the second part of his letter he proposed a blueprint for the next book. He said, "You should write a second volume and in it treat three subjects in particular. 1. Since you have been teaching for more than half a century [that was a shock to read, although it was accurate], tell us what you really think of American education, based on your own experience. 2. Then, rather than telling us more about authors you have met and observed, tell us about your parents, especially your father. 3. And third [the letter had almost the form of a French lecture], tell us what it means to be a believer today. Is your religious belief as real for you now as it was in earlier years?"

I took to heart those three topics, which I did try to develop in the second volume. Those topics and others, too. *Aubade: A Teacher's Notebook*, I would call a book essentially about teaching.

Since that time (1983), engaged in trying to write a third possible volume of recollections, I have become quite familiar with an emotion that seems to take over when I begin the writing of an episode in my life, or some reflection on the episode, or a portrait of an eminent person I may have encountered, or the portrait of an obscure person whom I know and like.

The most exact word I can find to describe the emotion is *panic*. Easy synonyms would be "fear" or "dread." But when to myself I try to name it, the word "panic" always comes first. Recently I began wondering about the origin, the etymology, of the word, and discovered that it may well come from Pan, the god Pan of Greek mythology. In my sketchy memory I had always thought of Pan as being a rollicking deity, associated with woods and fields and fertility. A semigod perhaps, part animal, with horns and hoofs, and the ears of a goat. A gifted musician also, who played on reeds or pipes named after him: *Pan pipes*.

But there my memory stopped, and I was not at all close to understanding why the word *panic* comes from Pan. A bit of research turned up a few suggestions that made sense of the word. It would seem to spring from the fear of travelers at night who believed they heard the sound of his pipes in the wilderness, an eerie menacing sound. His haunts were caves and mountains, wild places, although his favorite spot was Arcady, the Greek island where he was born, the offspring of Hermes (messenger of the gods) and a nymph. The fear instilled by the sound of his pipes is related, I presume, to the ugliness of Pan, which caused the nymphs he wooed in great numbers to reject him.

So, the emotion of panic and the shadow of Pan preside over many of these pages that I have written and am trying to write. In this life of a chronicler, of a man tracking down his past, wooing his past in order to exploit it, I have felt myself turning into a predatory animal-personality, not too far removed from Pan himself. In my own case, at least, the tension is always there in the need to write a work that will be at once confessional and reticent. If I defined the meaning of these two words in this context, I might call this need, this vocation, the desire to write about what may seem significant and even universal in any man's life, and to refrain from speaking of the trivial and the trite, of the infertile. Pan led a shoddy life in his lechery, and was at the same time a skilled musician.

In these efforts to recollect the past and to re-create it, to record particulars that may stir the imagination of a reader, I start quite deliberately on this third round with the word *sites*, that is, with places that retain for me very special atmospheres.

Like Pan, I never lived on Olympus. The Olympian gods despised Pan for his simplicity. After all, he was only a disreputable old goat-legged Arcadian god. On one occasion Apollo beat Pan in a musical contest. But Apollo had a seven-stringed lyre, whereas Pan had fashioned his pipes from uneven reeds he had found growing out of marsh water. He had been chasing a nymph, Syrinx, and she had been magically metamorphosed into the reeds. So, in a way, the playing on the pipes was a substitute for lovemaking. Art is that, I suppose, a higher form of living, a means of grasping what a man has lived or has not lived. And "panic" is a mental state induced by god Pan whenever I begin a search, not with musical notes, but with words, for some clearer vision of the past.

Every life is mysterious. No one can really see anyone else's life, unless it is written about. But when it is being written about, and then possibly read later, it inevitably turns into allegory, into some form of figurative plausibility. It is not quite fiction, but it is not very far from fiction. Today some of the leading works of modern literature are called autobiographical fiction or fictional autobiography. Moreover, they are studied as belonging to that special genre: *David Copperfield* by Dickens, *A Portrait of the Artist as a Young Man* by James Joyce, *Remembrance of Things Past* by Proust, *Sons and Lovers* by D. H. Lawrence, and more recently, *Portnoy's Complaint* by Philip Roth, and *Herzog* by Saul Bellow.

A simple sentence in Yeats's *Autobiography* says more to me than most learned disquisitions on the art of autobiography: "It is myself that I remake." At first one lives, one is concerned with the act of living, and then writing takes over. A few years ago, an autobiographer might easily have called his work a reconstruction of his life, the writer's self-picturing. But today a more exact term, taken from the new criticism, would be "deconstruction." This word, as used by the critics, would seem to mean that the true self of a man is always displaced in language.

We might contrast in terms of length Marcel Proust's very long novel-autobiography, *Remembrance of Things Past*, with Jean-Paul Sartre's brief auto-biography, *Les Mots*, and yet find in each, in the elaborately conceived and written fiction of Proust and in the few pages of the philosopher, the same goal, the same conclusions: the account of how a man, in writing about his life, becomes a stranger to himself. Writing is indeed a process of self-alteration. Living belongs to the past. Writing is the present.

Each new autobiographer, as he joins a long succession of others, sees the foolishness of what he is doing: this curious escape from life into words, this leap from an intention (to depict this episode and that episode) to the expression of the intention. Because of this foolishness, most are only part-time autobiographers: Saint Augustine was, after all, primarily a theologian; Cellini, a goldsmith and sculptor; Rousseau, a philosophe; Gide, a novelist; O'Casey, a playwright; Thomas Merton, the author of mystical writings. In most cases, the autobiography is the book standing apart from the principal books, an adjunct book, an exercise book on the somewhat shameful art of confession.

It is hard to discover a history of the form, the genre of autobiography, as it appears through the centuries. And yet history is everywhere in the finest examples of autobiography. Each one finds its own shape thanks in part to the history of the day in which it was written, and thanks especially to the personality of the writer.

Almost any two autobiographies, chosen at random, will demonstrate worlds of difference in content and tone and degree of self-revelation: the unfinished *Autobiography*, for example, of Benjamin Franklin, and *The Summing Up* by Somerset Maugham. In the major works of autobiography there is apparent a fundamental frustration. No one has been able to write the final chapter of his life, namely, his death. That account, which would be revealing, has never been included. This means that every autobiography is by definition unfinished.

Throughout my life, I have been attached deeply to very few people. But I have been interested in and attracted to many, because of whom and through whom I have tried to understand my own feelings, hopes, motivations. In my meetings with famous or almost famous people, I have learned very little. I have learned a great deal from their work—but that is something else. In their role of human beings they tend to be (and perhaps have to be) masks. Obscure and humble people are far richer in their simplicity than famous people in their visible masks. The character of a fellow pumping gasoline into my car, or the character of a waitress serving me my soup and sandwich, or my twenty-year-old student reading Proust for the first time, is more exciting to me than the character of a United States senator, or even of a president of the United States. The gift of speech in senators and presidents does not often accompany the power of thought.

We can't always encounter heroes in our life, but we do encounter and are excited to observe traces of the heroic in those people we meet in our daily life. The hero is an important term (possibly the most important) in literary study, and I learn about him not only in the stories of Aeneas and Julien Sorel, but in the lives of humble people that touch mine. In the historical-literary sense, we learned in the middle of the twentieth century a great deal about the hero as he is explained in two books: *Myth of the Birth of the Hero* by Otto Rank, published in 1910, and *The Hero of a Thousand Faces* by Joseph Campbell, published in

1940. They emphasize the famous formula that the hero is the man who passes from a lowly state at his birth to an exalted state at the end of his life. The story of Moses illustrates this theory which today seems more than a theory. A mythic story, after all, ends by revealing truth.

Ulysses did not write his life story, nor did Moses, nor did Jesus of Nazareth. But Saint Augustine did, and Henry Thoreau did, and the pattern of the heroic is in them, at times strongly, and at times faintly. One man lives his life, and another man writes it. It is the same man. The one who lived and the one who writes: two persons in the same body.

As the events in an autobiography form a pattern, it may appear to be prose fiction. At least it uses all the devices a novel does: characters and the chronicle of a family, maxims and lyric passages, confessions and narrative. In trying to trace its history, critics claim that Saint Augustine invented the form, and Rousseau made it into a modern type of literary expression. But one might move back earlier in history, to Petronius and his *Satyricon*, and today to the Protean form of autobiography add Federico Fellini's films, such as *Amarcord*. And why not the self-portraits of Van Gogh and Chagall as well as those of Rembrandt and Georges Rouault? In 1984 the Martha Graham Dance Company revived in New York City several of the earlier Graham dances. One of them, *Deaths and Entrances*, I remembered from the 1950s, when Martha Graham herself danced it. We learned then that the work was about the three Brontë sisters. In 1984 we knew that it was also about Martha Graham and her two sisters: an autobiographical dance.

Rousseau uses the first person pronoun in his *Confessions*. The famous opening sentence tells it all: "I want to show to mankind a man in the total truth of his nature, and that man is me" (*et cet homme ce sera moi*). Henry Adams, in his *Education*, uses the third person: "Under the shadow of Boston State House, in 1838, a child was born: Henry Brooks Adams." Saint Augustine uses the second person in addressing his confessions to God: "I came upon you in the chambers of my memory."

The use of memory, indispensable to autobiography, is a recycling of memories, both conscious and subconscious aspects of living, by means of which a life story may be transformed into a personal myth. Without the writer realizing it, images return in this recycling, persistently return, and provide, if a reader considers them carefully, a clue to the man's obsessions, to his drives and goals, no matter how secret the goals are to himself and to others. Even more than images, there is usually visible in an autobiography a grouping of scenes or episodes, a pattern of a life unlike any other life, which gives its distinction to each autobiography. These images and these patterns reveal the identity of the writer, to himself first, and then to a reader. This identity, reached through words, is new to the writer and is new to his friends, to all who believed they knew him.

It is no longer reasonable to claim that Saint Augustine invented autobiography. However, a case may be made for his having invented the spiritual autobiography. The *Confessions*, a title indicating a sense of guilt, does stand at the head of a long list of books where the life of a man is presented as mythic, through a series of vignettes, of disparate scenes and materials, of geographical changes, at the end of which a significant form emerges.

Anthony Trollope once wrote: "In our lives we are always weaving novels." This thought has been expressed in many varying ways. Thomas Wolfe, closer to us than Trollope, has said: "All serious work in fiction is autobiographical." Most autobiographies or autobiographical novels seem to be apologies, testaments of defiance, but also of dedication. In the preface to his *Essais*, Montaigne wrote his famous sentence: *Je suis moi-même la matière de mon livre.* John Florio, in 1603, translated those words as: "Myself am the ground work of my book."

Let me offset these rather dogmatic or doctrinal quotations with a brief sentence of Ernest Renan, the nineteenth-century French historian and philosopher who wrote in his book about his childhood and adolescence: *Souvenirs d'enfance et de jeunesse: Ce qu'on dit de soi est toujours poésie.* ("What one says of oneself is always poetry.") Of all the statements of this nature that I have come across, the most awesome, the most definitive, is by Oscar Wilde: "All artistic creation is absolutely subjective."

Now, these sentences contradict what I was taught by the first group of so-called "new critics" in the earlier part of the twentieth century when I was in college. They taught us to trust the tale rather than the teller of the tale. They taught us to look upon a story or a poem as an object, an artifact that has little to do with the place where it was written, or the time when it was written, or indeed the personality of the man who wrote it. And yet, despite this stern doctrine, I find that the desire for self-portraiture is in evidence everywhere. Self-portraiture may well be a synonym of self-knowledge. That admonition to know oneself comes to us from the Greek philosophers. The loftiest interpretation given to this advice in our English tradition is in Cardinal Newman, in the "apology" he wrote for his life (*Apologia Pro Vita Sua*), where he says: "Self-knowledge is the source of man's knowledge of God."

Perhaps the best approach to this problem of definition might be to use the word *subjectivity* rather than *autobiography*, and then analyze the leading forms that subjectivity takes in literature. The autobiographical novel would come first: *A Portrait of the Artist as a Young Man* by Joyce, for example. Then the personal poem: *The Prelude* of Wordsworth, or the sonnets of Shakespeare. And then finally the formal self-history such as *The Education of Henry Adams*.

At best it is an elusive genre. All language of the self is that. In our secular world of the twentieth century the word "self" has replaced the word "soul." Most of the theorists today would say that memory is the core of selfhood. Saint Augustine has often been called *the* philosopher of memory. He calls memory "an inner chamber, vast and unbounded."

Several centuries later, Rousseau secularized Saint Augustine's Christian introspection, in emphasizing in his *Confessions* childhood and adolescence. He was the first of the aggressive young men coming up from the provinces to the capital: Eugène de Rastignac of Balzac and Julien Sorel of Stendhal.

As the genre developed in the nineteenth and twentieth centuries, the writer and the speaker became one person. The life of a man is always larger than the book he writes about his life. From the opening lines he writes, the autobiographer knows that all is approximate. And the reason is the language he has to use. Language is opaque.

Henry Thoreau died at the age of forty-four. In his *Walden*, he wrote a book that is still read today, and especially by youngsters, by young men who are thrilled by that life in the woods, by that hut close to the pond, by that independence of a man living close to nature and calling himself "inspector of snow-storms and rain-storms." When Thoreau is released from jail in the narrative, adolescent boys reading that passage today are captivated by such a sentence as:

> I returned to the woods in season
> to get my dinner of huckleberries
> on Far Haven Hill.

Walden is indeed our Yankee substitute for *Robinson Crusoe*.

Henry Adams, on the other hand, and at the other extreme, is our most brilliant misanthrope. He forgets his misanthropy only when he is studying the medieval world. He is read today by older readers than the readers of Thoreau, and they are fascinated by his converting a family history into our national history, and by his awesome prophecy that modern technology will endanger the planet.

Adams's remarkable use of place-names guides the journey of his life through memory: Quincy, Boston, Washington, Harvard, Paris 1900, the White House under Theodore Roosevelt, the Bois de Boulogne, Mount Vernon Street in Boston.

Adams is primarily a historian, and therefore sees all of life moving into history. If I read Adams now, I am constantly reminded of Proust, not only in his use of place-names and in his evoking of the Middle Ages, but especially perhaps in the history he provides of an intellectual caste. Language for Adams, as it was for Proust, is the mold into which the past can fit. When he speaks of the naïveté of American politicians, I can recall comparable passages in Proust on Norpois and Brichot. Both Adams and Proust, at two moments in recent history, deplored the fact that those men who should lead by force of intellect and culture and tradition are no longer in charge.

This kind of writing I am discussing, we tend to call a diary when we are very young. It is usually an account of what happened and what we thought about what happened. As we get older, we tend to call it a journal, indicating thereby that we are writing at greater length about certain events, certain years, and trying to make something out of them, something even historical. The French use the term *journal* as a close synonym of history: Amiel, Stendhal, Gide. And then, when one reaches a venerable age, one tends to write *confessions* and *autobiography*. At such an age one has the right to be less discreet.

There are very marked, almost national traits of autobiographies written in America, from early Colonial days right up to Norman Mailer and Malcolm X. Two have reached the status of classics: *Walden* and *The Education of Henry Adams*. In most American autobiographies attention is paid to the life of the nation as well as to the life of the man writing his life. And often puzzling questions are asked, such as: What is America? Who are Americans? Unlike the French, the Italians and the Germans, Americans are immigrants, from all countries. This has led F. Scott Fitzgerald to say in his posthumously published book, *The Crack-up*, "America is not a land and not a people. It is an idea." Fitzgerald discovered in writing this passage an even more striking way of expressing this "idea" of America, when he wrote: "France was a land, England was a people, but America was a willingness of the heart."

Readers of autobiography are often therapy seekers. In the *Confessions* of Rousseau there is an outrageous passage in which he sees himself standing before the throne of the Almighty, on the day of judgment, with the book of his *Confessions* in his hand and reading it to the whole of assembled humanity. Behind this picture Rousseau is asking a question of his readers: "Is anyone better than me?" And behind that question is the belief of the *philosophe*: we are all equally bad, made bad by society.

The new critics today have taken up avidly the study, the criticism, of autobiography. These are the critics who study intensively and somewhat exclusively the language of a book, and especially the language that seems to them to come from the subconscious of the writer. They are guided by their conviction that the writer is not one subject. He is on the contrary a multiplicity of subjects. This belief leads the critic to ask, as he asks more and more often these days, "Who is speaking in the text?" And even the more basic question: "What is an author?"

The key terms that Freud made familiar to all of us—repression, narcissism, and the unconscious—are strong clues to the self of a man, constituted by a discourse, by words that the self never completely masters. The critic of the self to which an autobiographer has to return over and over again as he writes, is an elusive center because it is covered up and concealed in the unconscious. The new critic is very much bent on discovering, if not the unconscious, at least traces of the unconscious as they appear in the text. Every text for this new kind of searcher we still call a critic, appears to him as an articulation of the relations between texts. Every text is therefore a product of intertextuality.

The word "autobiography" was first used at the end of the eighteenth century. Prior to that time the terms had been "memoirs," "confessions," "personal journals." Memory is the point of departure. It is that faculty in us that remembers things. But memory is not always total or dependable. In the writing of one's memoirs, it is supported by a second faculty, imagination. Imagination alters those things that memory recalls. The images created by the imagination are fact and fiction intermingled, one supporting and explaining the other.

In addressing his *Confessions* to God, Saint Augustine, who was a great stylist, knew that God is omniscient and had no need of his life story. But his readers did. The past is narrated in an autobiography, but it is written in the present for a present and future audience. Two strangely contrasting connivances therefore: the connivance between author and his past; and the connivance between an author and his reader.

Little wonder that autobiography has engendered more definitions to explain it than any other genre. Little wonder that panic may be present whenever a self-portrait is being sketched, because no matter what the profession is of the sketcher—poet or soldier, monk or novelist, statesman or actress—in the sketch there will be discernible elements of history and art, of fiction and fact. There will be ideas that came from the era in which the man lived.

The source of that panic that often takes over the writer's feelings is possibly in the conflict between the two lives he is trying to narrate and join: the life that others saw him live and the life known only to himself. They are related, those two lives, and it is the art of the writer that relates them.

The audience of a writer—and I believe this is especially true for biography and autobiography—is composed in part of voyeurs, thieves, parasites.

They read—and that means they walk off with whatever they feel is worth taking. This is an ancient habit belonging to the world of literature as well as to other art worlds: painting, dance, architecture. In some versions of mythology, Apollo himself is made to look like an unimaginative bully and boor. In fact, in some tales, he stole from Pan, the god or the goat who got there first.

There is today a polite term, an erudite term designating such thefts: "intertextuality." But since the writer (whether he be poet or autobiographer) is the instrument of culture, such thefts are forgiven, and, like Pan, he is free to remain the rebel, the singer who shocks his community and even terrifies, through occasional excesses, those who hear him. At first the community will tend to exclude him from the tribal dance. In modern times they have done that with Osip Mandelstam in Russia, with Federico Garcia Lorca in Spain, with Arthur Rimbaud in France, and in America with Walt Whitman, with Henry Miller, and with other Panlike figures.

1. Sites

This text: my salvation.

The word is not too strong as I consider my efforts during the past two or three years to write the various chapters that follow in this book. They are all "sites," places where I have lived briefly or for some time, and which have continued through the years to retain for me atmospheres and dramas associated with people I have known and loved.

So I call this text my salvation, because in it, by means of words, I have restored myself. Almost as a building is restored, brick by brick, wall by wall. I have written the inventory of those who once surrounded me in the past, and of those who surround me today. Often I fail to distinguish between past and present, because of the reality of the past as it reforms in words, and because of the unreality of the present so finely compounded of the past and the future.

When I write in the silence of my house, I am multiplied into those selves that have lived in other houses, in other landscapes. Everything in the world seems to become a spectacle. My mission is perhaps that of surviving as witness to the eternity of those moments I remember as scenes of action or, quite simply, of meditation. As an oak tree grows, it becomes one with everything else in the universe. Its death is impossible to imagine.

These notes are in reality notations on my past as it was lived in a series of constantly changing settings. The shadows cast by those sites permitted me to see, or in some cases, not to see, what I could touch close at hand, and what I could discern at some distance. Today the shadows cast on me come from the years, from time and not from places, and it is a new kind of fecundity they provide. This I have learned to call in my mind the liturgy of writing. With the appearance of each dawn, of each *aube*, I ask, "How can I capture one word, one phrase?"

Let me say at the outset: this has been my most refractory book. And let me add: that is a good thing. I who love words feel I fabricate with them. Most days of my life begin with words spoken in a classroom. That has always been for me a privilege. As I move in and out of classrooms, I refresh my stagnancy. The other major help in living is diary-writing which permits me to loosen the ligatures. When revising time comes—the chillest part of this business of writing—I am at a low ebb with the book, because I know at that moment that poetry is the true history and not the seeming history of prose. Yes, poems are the true history, the true "story"; and that is why I turn back again and again to: "Among school children," "Burnt Norton," "Le pitre châtié," "La servante au grand coeur." Prose, in its greatest instances, gives me, not a story —that always seems inconsequential—but the reality of other human beings: La duchesse de Guermantes, Fabrice, Stephen Dedalus, Ishmael. Only in Dante do I find the dual and equal power of narrative and characters, of prose and poetry. The fiery tomb of Farinata is as real as his fiery spirit rising out of it.

Sites. Their number in my life and their variety have made me into a sala-mander. I have lived contentedly—and at times joyously—in all of them. How different they have been! Saint-Paul-de-Vence, for example, where I lived twice, each time for a month, in two different seasons, one warm June and one cold February.

The town itself, perched high above the Mediterranean, and classified in its entirety as a monument, since it was founded and built by François Premier, was the site. But in the center of the town I lived in the most comfortable hotel I have known, La Résidence, owned by the town's mayor, M. Marius, and serving in its spacious dining room, day after day, the most delectable meals I have eaten. Every other day at least I walked to La Fondation Maeght to enjoy and study the paintings there. They were naturally exhibited on the walls inside the museum. But outside in the small park extending from the entrance gate to the museum was a world by itself inhabited by statues . . . human forms, yes, recognizably human, but also not human, a race apart recalling the human race and another race, created by Alberto Giacometti. The park was a few trees, spaced at some distance from one another, and rivaling the almost tree-like dark bronze statues growing out of the ground, and existing like trees under the sun and the rain, under the cold of winter and the heat of summer.

Those figures, so expressive and attenuated, seemed to me more alive than the trees. I had seen the works of a sculptor grouped together inside a museum —Michelangelo in the Academia in Florence, Rodin in his Paris museum— but I had never seen a large number of the works of one man so placed in a garden-park as to give the impression of life going on, of moving bronzes. Their elongated figures, so fragile in their Mediterranean setting, that I wondered—it was hard not to ask such a question—if they had moved in their tentative stances outside of time and space as we know them.

As I returned day after day to walk for twenty minutes or so among the Giacometti statues, I would say to myself with more and more assurance: this is indeed the picture of man's tenuous existence. I knew their bronze was heavy and solid, and yet Giacometti had made them into figures threatened with being obliterated by the surrounding space. The distortion of their forms and their pervasive melancholy reminded me of human beings who have stalked me in nightmares. With each return visit to the Fondation Maeght I grew more familiar with my dreams and with the characters of Samuel Beckett's plays, with Vladimir and Estragon, with Hamm and Clov. In the literal sense, Giacometti from Switzerland, and Beckett from Ireland, were friends, but their art would have joined them in any case. Two exiles in France, working as artists in France, as Picasso from Spain and Apollinaire from Rome had worked a generation or two earlier. That other exile, from Russia, Marc Chagall, was even then living and painting in a house near the Fondation Maeght. I would see his smiling face from time to time as he entertained friends in the outside restaurant of La Colombe d'Or, the hotel opposite La Résidence.

A few years later a new French restaurant was announced as opening in Pittsboro, North Carolina, twenty-five miles from Durham. La Résidence was its name. I was invited to dinner there by some friends who knew the two owners, husband and wife. The young husband was the chef and I was introduced to him in the kitchen where he was in the midst of preparing a special dish. I apologized for bothering him, but had wanted to say that I had lived once at La Résidence in Saint-Paul and had enjoyed the fine cooking there. He was delighted to answer: "That is where I served as apprentice-cook and learned my profession. I named my own restaurant after it." Pittsboro (North Carolina) and Saint-Paul-de-Vence (Alpes Maritimes): sites of sybaritic indulgence.

Another dining room—but not a restaurant—in a girls' college in Vermont, where I was responsible for French literature in the "literature division," is a permanent picture in my memory. My first year there—it must have been 1936—in my ardor as a young teacher, I accepted the suggestion of my freshman group to have a "French table" every Monday lunch. Seven girls and myself around a large table in the corner of one of the smaller dining rooms, at a large window through which the sunlight flooded the table at exactly 12:30.

I had had one morning a two-hour class and two one-hour tutorials. The walk from the "barn," where my office was, to the Commons building of Bennington College revived me, and the change of pace, from teaching and advising, to eating and relaxed conversation, revived me too. I knew most of the girls at the table who were from my classes, but there were usually one or two new girls, French-speaking, and curious to test out the new French teacher. After a few Mondays I realized it was wise to have a subject or two in readiness that might help the conversation. The girls ate well, and steadily, and thus I ate less, in order to keep some kind of talk going on.

Everything seemed to be in a circle: the round table, the round plates, the round circle of heads—beautiful heads they were, with hair of all shades and all designs—and circular bits of conversation moving from one of us to the other as we reviewed the morning classes and the morning news from the outside world. Then, nostalgically, we reviewed memories of France, erratic memories we contributed as offerings to the conversation: Mont Saint-Michel, la Place de la Concorde, un café-crème aux Deux Magots, Chartres (which we often called the most vivid memory of all).

At this particular lunch—we were well into the fall term—when conversation was dragging, I pulled out one of the topics I had stored away for an emergency: our birthplaces and what we remembered of them. I began with myself and Brookline, Massachusetts. The girl to my left took it up easily and it continued round the table. I sensed quite early in the game that the girl to my right, who would be the last to name her birthplace and comment on it, was embarrassed and wanted the game to stop. I did my best to change the subject before it reached her, but the others became aware of this girl's hesitancy, and they, in a not unusual wave of cruelty, bore down on her. I was unable to save her. Her time came, and, blushing, she announced: "Je suis née à Oshkosh, Wisconsin, mais j'ai été conçue à Vienne." ("I was born in Oshkosh, but I was conceived in Vienna.") What eloquent brave words they were! We all responded with hilarity. It was her only visit to the French table.

That early memory of Bennington is the sun as its light hit the table, turning it into a reduplication of roundness, and the lightness, the deftness of the French language by which the eight of us moved into a small planet cut off from all the other round and square planets in that dining room. When the conversation went smoothly, we floated in an orbit of our own as if we were looking down at the state of Vermont and were determined to remain far above it in a temporary flight that was both escape and rejuvenation.

On the floor above that dining room in the Commons was the theater occupying most of the floor. There was a stage, with fairly good lighting equipment, and a backstage for dressing rooms. The house had a seating capacity of two to three hundred movable chairs. The theater was used for everything: plays, of course, in which I, as the years rolled by, had many small or big parts, concerts, lectures, dance classes, meetings of all kinds. As I think back on my Bennington years, I was always climbing up or coming down those two flights of stairs. Of all the performances I rehearsed and played in, and of all the meetings I attended, through the seventeen years I taught at the college, one more vividly than all the others is fixed in my memory, enshrined there in its setting of the theater, packed to the doors, when on the stage I stood beside André Malraux, introducing him at first, and then translating paragraph by paragraph what he said in French to an awestruck youthful audience.

It was 1936 or 1937. The time of the Spanish Civil War. Sponsored by the *Nation*, Malraux had come to this country to speak, on behalf of the Loyalists, at a large number of colleges and universities, and collect from his audiences as much money as he could for the anti-Franco cause. The excitement over having him for an hour or two in our small college community came from the cause he represented and from his stature as an eminent writer, at the time one of the best-known of living French authors. *La Condition Humaine* (*Man's Fate*), on China's uprising in 1922, in particular was read in most colleges. He was the "engaged" writer, long before Sartre was to make the word *engagé* into a literary battle cry. He stood midway between the international fame of André Gide, as it had developed between 1925 and 1935, and the international fame of the existentialist Jean-Paul Sartre, as it developed between 1940 and 1950.

Margaret Marshall of the *Nation* was in charge of Malraux's itinerary. Bennington had given her my name as the "French teacher" who would introduce Malraux and translate his speech. She and the president of the college, Robert Leigh, had asked me to pick up Malraux at the Albany station and drive him to Bennington. He would be coming by train from New York. As I drove that late morning to Albany, I reviewed in my mind what I knew of his activities, most of which were shrouded in mystery: his role in China, his archaeological mission in Laos, the prix Goncourt in 1933 for *La Condition Humaine*, his participation in the conflict in Spain. After the victory in 1918

Malraux had guessed more clearly than most the future of communism. He had quite literally lived various phases of recent history with abundant courage and intelligence.

My growing nervousness as I waited for his train to pull into the Albany station was dissipated with his first words, the casualness of his greeting, and perhaps by his own tensions and tics. He almost never smiled, but there was warmth in his words. We were alone in my car for the drive between Albany and Bennington, and I tried to say to him in my fumbling sentences how unexpected, how unusual, this meeting was for me. I could tell that he was already worn out from those visits to colleges, from other drives from station to college with other unknown drivers.

In the eyes of the younger generation in France, Malraux was *un maître*, the outstanding leader at the moment. I tried to tell him, without flattery, that I was aware of this, that I was not simply a chauffeur. At the beginning it was hard for him to be more than perfunctory, and not until I asked him what he was working on at that time in his literary life did he become animated and seemingly eager to talk. "I am writing on art," he said, "on the psychology of art. And if I am able to continue with it, it will be a large work, my life work perhaps."

I had not seen any formal announcement of such a study. Malraux assured me that there had not been an announcement, that it was still a secret. He wanted to get farther into the subject, especially into the subject of primitive art, before allowing any such title as *La psychologie de l'art* to be used, and especially any such title as *Les Voix du silence*. He spoke lucidly, volubly about his new subject, as he smoked cigarette after cigarette without the slightest pause between.

Malraux was a dazzling, almost bewildering speaker. Some years later I came upon a short passage in Gide's *Journal* where he speaks of dining alone with Malraux and feeling mortified by the man's brilliance, by his intelligence (*Journal*, 5 septembre 1936). On the stage in Bennington Malraux demonstrated less of that and more of his histrionic powers, of his willful crusade for justice. The novelist-art critic easily turned diplomat and emissary. He pleaded for the Spanish Loyalists, and only at the end, when his voice broke, did he allow his emotions to be felt. I was hard put to retain all he put in a paragraph of his discourse, and I often ruthlessly condensed his points. Elsa Hirsch, one of the painters at Bennington, helped me from the front row where she sat, when my memory faltered. Once Malraux turned to me and said to the audience, "J'ai donné à mon ami un devoir infernal."

During all the subsequent years of my teaching at Bennington, when I was on that stage of the college theater, in rehearsals and performances of many plays, it remained for me, and still does, the stage where André Malraux spoke so fervently. Mine was a minor role that day, a servant's role in reality, but one that a young teacher of French literature has cherished throughout the rest of his life.

A third site—not in Vermont, but in New York City—is nevertheless related to Bennington. Kathy Henry was an infrequent visitor to the French table on Mondays. I was always pleased to have her there because of her pure French accent. She was a shy girl, and not until I discovered that she spoke easily and intelligently about acting and the theater was I able to involve her in the general conversation. She came from New York City. We often met at mass at the Ecole du Sacré Coeur church in Bennington. Religious practice was a central part of her life. I introduced her to one of the drama fellows, Chandler Cowles, who had come to Bennington to work with Francis Fergusson. He was attracted to the Church, and the three of us would drive into Bennington on Sundays in the same car. The Church and the theater: how closely interrelated they became in our conversation! It happened from time to time that the three of us were cast in the same play.

Invited by Kathy, we also met in New York, in her parents' large apartment on East 72nd Street. I never saw the end of that apartment. It stretched out in every direction, beautifully furnished, cared for by servants who seemed to obey the directions of Mr. Henry. The chairs were French and the tapestries covering them were French. Mrs. Henry seemed shy and retiring. In the bits of conversation we had, I found her intelligent and sincerely, profoundly devout, a daily communicant in the French church of Saint-Jean Baptiste in the nearby East 70s. I yearned to know her better, to talk with her at greater length. But she was self-effacing and self-critical. I thought of her as a Guermantes noble lady. In her presence I imagined her to be Madame de Marsantes, Robert's mother in Proust's novel. Kind, almost too kind to Kathy and Chandler, to me, to the servants, she would appear suddenly and then disappear before we could really engage her.

Mr. Henry was seldom at home. He was affable when he did join us, but affable to such an extreme that it seemed he was trying to make up for his absences. On Chandler in particular he bestowed physical signs of comradeship: hugs and backslappings. He too was a Guermantes, the duc Basin, I thought most of the time, and at slightly sinister moments, the duc's brother, le baron de Charlus. The world of that apartment, where all the doors of all the rooms were always kept closed, was the most Proustian world I had yet encountered. It was a salon, and I watched it as if it were the stage of a theater where the actions of the characters were never totally clear, where plots seemed to be building up but never reached a climax.

One decade later, when I had to spend a few days in New York, Kathy insisted I use one of their guest rooms. She promised: no entertaining, total freedom to come and go, to do the writing I was working on that week in early spring. So, I lived in my own quarters, but with the sense of the mysterious house all about me, more than ever the observer and not the participant.

I was trying to write a study of Proust's novel and working especially on Mme Swann's appearances in the Bois de Boulogne, on scenes where she walked quite fast along the Allée des Acacias, and others where she passed in her open carriage, and acknowledged the bows of the gentlemen on foot, all members of the Jockey Club.

Those mornings I rose very early, at dawn, to walk in Central Park. Seventy-second Street led to Fifth Avenue, and beyond it to a path cutting across the park from east to west, with an open field on both sides. Usually I was alone on that morning jaunt, but one morning, as I reached the park, I saw far ahead of me, coming toward me on the path, the figure of a woman. She was walking steadily at a good pace. The scene was so similar to the pages I was working on in Proust, that I jokingly to myself called that figure Mme Swann who was confusing Central Park with the Bois de Boulogne. If she continued walking on that path, we would have to pass in close proximity, and I began wondering: "Will she greet me, will she at least say hello?" We were totally alone in a vast space under the sky that bore the first color of dawn. I could soon make out a broad-brimmed floppy hat on the woman's head and imagined that perhaps I would not even see her face when we collided, only to separate as we continued in our different directions.

When we did pass, the brim of the hat flopped up and I saw her face. It was Greta Garbo wearing dark glasses, and totally oblivious to my presence. The face was still beautiful, but there was sternness in it as she began walking a bit faster. She must have feared some word from me, some interference in her solitary morning exercise. I was of course disappointed, but also elated at seeing not Odette Swann but Greta Garbo. And ever since that Central Park vision, whenever I discuss that passage in my Proust class, I see the face of Mme Swann as that of the great actress.

Two decades later Kathy Cowles with her two young sons, Christopher and Matthew, came to Bennington to spend a few days with me in my apartment in Bingham House. Young Christopher was my godson. The boys were curious about the Vermont college setting where their mother and father had met, curious about me who seemed to know a great deal about their family, curious about a college: a place, after all, where ordinary human beings lived.

Kathy and I enjoyed showing our old haunts to the boys, especially the college theater where Kathy once played Jocaste to my Oedipe in Cocteau's *La Machine Infernale*. We showed them the pew in the Church of the Sacré Coeur where Chandler, Kathy, and I sat for mass and where we listened to the Canadian-French sermons of le Père Campeau. We showed them the site of the Mayflower Inn where Chandler and I lived for one year and where we carried on late at night our best bull sessions on the theater, on Francis Fergusson, on Kathy Henry, on the 72nd Street apartment, on the mysterious manners of Mrs. Henry, and on the equivocal behavior of Mr. Henry.

I shore up my emotions when I think of times and sites. More and more they impinge one on the other, and reveal to me connections—metaphysical connections—I would never have thought of when I lived on those sites. Or if I had made the connections, I would have seen them as signs of neurosis. They emerge for me now, not only in the words that I write, but in the authentic dreams that take me over in the very earliest hours of the new day. More and more am I solitary in a literal autobiographical sense, and more and more am I inhabited by voices and phantoms and sites. I now fully occupy the spirit and the body of that solitary figure I was at my birth. Solitary, yes, but filled with so many names, and eager to search for the names of those I cannot name. That search at times turns into a torment, as it does now when a sharp-featured face of a woman returns to me in my dreams whom I know and cannot name, whom I cannot attach to any decade in my life. Her face is birdlike, ambiguous, old. Is she one or is she a composite face guarding and warning me? Is she Oriane de Guermantes? Have I created her out of many others? She has a serene countenance. But she is also enigmatically smiling as if she were saying to me: "Human lives do not last. They are far too egoistic!"

Sites. I have lived in them and I continue to live in them. I am an unfettered nomad. The dreams that propel me through so many places and so much space, through so many wearying familiar phenomena, dissipate when I leave my house in the morning and see the sun in a sky of unflecked light blue. At that moment I know the perils of my soul to be formless.

Sites: the theater at Bennington where Malraux spoke, the Giacometti bronzes in Saint-Paul-de-Vence, the path across Central Park where I passed by a great actress whom I had taken to be Mme Swann walking in the Bois de Boulogne. My life imitates a book, many books. The pages of a book are my mobility as I move from site to site. I have lived through and by the ceremony of language. I am a life transformed into text.

This text: my salvation.

2. Popham Beach, Maine

It is among the earliest of my memories, rich in memories of smells, of sights, of food, and above all of a way of living that was totally exotic for me in my eighth, ninth, and tenth years when each summer I spent two weeks there in the month of August. Popham Beach. To say those two words today in my seventy-fourth year is to conjure up a vision of wonderment and delight, of a first experience of living away from home in a world different from Brookline, Massachusetts. Those six weeks of my childhood proved to me that the world was indeed vast and diverse, and that summertime, August in particular, could be a reward for good behavior and studiousness during the other months of the year.

Those three summer vacations—real vacations, not just releases from school—I owed to Aunt Polly, secretary to the superintendent of the Brookline schools. She spent the entire month of August at Popham, every August through all my childhood and adolescence. My unmarried aunt, Miss Mary Adams, was the only member of my family free to leave Brookline for an entire month to breathe the salt air of Maine and walk at a good gait the long board walk that ran from the Riverside Hotel to South Beach. I had heard many stories about Popham Beach before I went there, the ones I liked the best concerning the red jacket my aunt wore only at Popham. The natives of the small town used to say: "It must be August. There's Polly Adams' red coat."

I felt proud that my aunt was so well-known at Popham, where I watched her on our arrival being greeted by some who worked at the Riverside Hotel, and by a few of the guests there who, like her, came every year from Boston and Rhode Island and even as far away as New York. Later, at Percy and Stacey General Store where we went to buy such things as toothpaste, she would be welcomed back into the community, not merely as a familiar customer but as a faithful friend. They made of me a bit, as the young nephew, but I knew Aunt Polly had prepared that by her August fidelity. She had carefully explained to me that people in Maine are suspicious of those who come from outside, and that it takes a little time to be accepted by them. Being a relative of one already accepted, I never felt unwanted or scorned. I did not have to make my way by myself.

I enjoyed the two return trips more than the first because then I too was recognized ("He's growing fast, young Wallace," or "He'll soon be as tall as you, Miss Polly"). Best of all, I recognized places and people, and even heard myself explaining the wonders of Popham Beach to newcomers. There were four major points of interest about which I became as learned as I was enthusiastic: Fort Popham, to the left on leaving the hotel; the Coast Guard Station to the right at the end of the long boardwalk; South Beach beyond that; and best of all for me, the Riverside Hotel itself. I never acknowledged that preference when I was actually there, because I knew I was supposed to prefer the other three. The hotel was for eating and sleeping. Aunt Polly constantly urged me to stay outside and keep breathing deeply the salt air that came to us from the ocean and the mouth of the Kennebec River. At the end of each breakfast we walked up and down the long piazza of the hotel and breathed noisily synchronizing our intake and output (Today when my doctor tells me during a medical checkup to take a deep breath, I am transported back to the piazza of the Riverside Hotel as I followed the instructions of my aunt in her frequently assumed role of athletic coach.) That early in the morning, the rocking chairs on the piazza were still unoccupied, the sun had begun rising behind the hotel, and that morning walk was my favorite when there was no sun on me, no sand under me, and a dining room, visible through the windows, that was gradually filling up with hotel guests.

After the exercises of walking and breathing, my aunt spent a part of each day lying in the sun on South Beach. It seemed to stretch out for miles along the ocean front, this natural, sandy, beautifully formed beach. It was practically wild because there were very few cottages lining it, and very few hotel guests and townspeople using it. But every day in August when there was sun, Aunt Polly, whose skin tanned easily, was there, with a book or two, and a pillow for her head. Relaxation and brief naps on the beach were part of her summer regimen. Almost no one went swimming because of the strong undertow and the extreme cold of the water. I dipped into the water every day but stayed close to the shore and enjoyed being vigorously toweled after a few minutes of pretending to swim. Since my skin easily burned, I cut short the morning and afternoon visits to the beach and made off for shadier spots.

The nearest was the Coast Guard Station where the two men in charge allowed me to examine the large rowboats and the rescue equipment they maintained in good condition. Popham had a long history of shipwrecks. Navigation into the mouth of the Kennebec River was hazardous. It was sixteen miles up river to Bath, and there was often danger from wind, fog, and tide. I was more impressed with the powers of the elements as I listened to the coast guard stories than with the loss of lives and property.

The two principal coast guards were friendly to me those three summers I paid them regular visits. They knew the history of the place and enjoyed rehearsing it. Each year they used me in one of their more impressive exercises. I was placed in a basket and shot out by means of a cable to a boat which they pretended was caught on a sand bank or wrecked on a reef. Thus I became one of their assistants, and thus I acquired information about Popham Beach. A riverside-seaside village, they called it, with its three miles of perfect beach.

I learned to check on details from their conversation, which almost always consisted of details of nature, terms and names that I would never encounter in Brookline or Boston where the natural world had been replaced with streets and parks and subways. They encouraged me to pick blueberries which grew in abundance, and even to go into the cranberry bogs and help out the pickers there. The blueberries were wild, but the cranberries were an industry in Popham. The men taught me how to look for sandpipers skittering along the beach at the waterline, and how to watch sea gulls and especially the friendly seals bobbing up and down close to shore. They told me about foghorns and I sometimes watched them repair bell buoys. I tried to enjoy, as they did, the smell of sweet grass and the mixed smell of salt air and pine. One early morning, before my hotel breakfast, they took me clamming at low tide in the bay.

All of these things were fresh and new to me, and each one an experience in itself. Today, so many years later, I can still see and hear and smell all those parts of Maine which the coast guards referred to so casually and which I seized upon as minor revelations: crushed clamshells on the walks around the hotel, the lapping of waves against the old wharf piling, the windswept dunes behind the village.

The Coast Guard Station was the first point of escape from my aunt in her languorous pose on South Beach where she covered the books (she seldom read) with her red jacket. The second point, where I was usually quite alone, was the Popham pier, at the end of the beach and close to the hotel and village. It extended a good distance into the water so that the big steamboat from Boston docked there even at low tide. I enjoyed walking to the end, when it was deserted, as much as when my aunt and I, with other hotel guests and people from the village, gathered there at those specific times morning and evening when the boat was docking or leaving. These were minor celebrations, welcoming the new arrivals or waving good-bye to those departing. On each occasion the boat was the central figure, and the captain who waved, too. "The Boston boat," as we all called it, was our bond with the civilization that filled our lives during the other parts of the year. We boarded the boat in the evening in Boston and reached Popham in early morning.

After leaving the wharf on my walks of investigation and prowling, I continued on in the direction of the hotel. At times I watched the tugboats and barges making for the mouth of the river or coming out from the river, and at other times when there was little to see on the water, I searched for arrowheads on the sand or on the land bordering the sand. Indians had lived there before George Popham arrived with the first English settlers thirteen years before the Pilgrims landed at Plymouth Rock.

The goal of this second part of my walk was the fort, a large granite Civil War fort on the point overlooking river and sea. It had been manned in the Civil War, in the Spanish-American War, and was to be manned briefly in World War I, soon after my last August visit.

There were many aspects to fire the imagination of a nine-year-old youngster: dark dungeons far below, and circular stairways leading to the top which appeared to me to be the top of the world. From there I could see a part of the river, and South Beach, which my coast guard friends had taught me was once called Hunnewell's Beach. Beyond the small village church I could see the bent forms of clam diggers in the bay. More inland I spotted berry patches everywhere, and cranberry bogs whose cranberries would be exported to Boston. Nearer to the fort, the familiar Riverside Hotel was spread with people playing croquet on the lawn, and close by the hotel I would check to see the General Store, and the boardwalk weaving its way toward the beach.

All of that was my new world spread out before me as I gazed over it each of those three summers from the top of Fort Popham. More than the fort itself, parts of which seemed sinister to me, I reveled in the view from the fort: sky and ocean and river, islands in the river, and lighthouses, pine trees, and river boats. My pedagogic coast guards, and, to a lesser extent, Aunt Polly, had taught me so much and in so few days that I felt bursting with knowledge and awareness. That other world of school in Brookline, of my parents at home, and of Boston—all of that was obliterated. I existed only in the wonders of the present. An overflow of feeling kept me there for many minutes while I walked over the summit of that stone fortress and surveyed the world in every direction. Each time I was caught in a spell I hesitated to break. I felt involved in some great pattern of life. During the time I was alone on the fort, I lived a timid, exhausted gratitude, to my aunt first for having invited me to come with her to Popham, and then to my parents for having brought me to into this miraculous existence.

Best of all, after South Beach, after the Coast Guard Station, after Fort Popham, was my return to the Riverside Hotel, to my small room there at the end of the long hallway on the second floor, and to all the other parts that were open to me: the lobby and the front desk, the parlor, the dining room, and the piazza. Wherever I went, there were people to speak to: guests or workers on the hotel staff. It was such a simple family-style hotel that there was little distinction, and certainly no class distinction, between guests and maids or waiters or cooks. All possible shyness in me was swept away by the sponta- neous friendliness of everyone who spoke to me. I knew I belonged more to the hotel than to the beach. Days of fog and dampness (there were not too many in August) delighted me, because then I had full permission to explore and enjoy the inside of the hotel, to encounter a variety of people young and old. Each one seemed to know who I was and what I was doing there, and if they didn't they quickly asked, and that was the beginning of a new acquain- tance. The Riverside Hotel marked the beginning of my social life, and many years later when I read the second volume of Proust's novel, *A l'ombre des jeunes filles en fleurs*, I knew that Popham was my Balbec and the old Riverside Hotel was le Grand Hôtel de Balbec.

They were worlds apart, my Popham and young Marcel's Balbec, conti- nents and social classes apart. The elaborate summertime life at a Normandy beach resort bore little resemblance to the rigid simplicity of Maine where no Mme de Villeparisis took me on carriage drives. Only "flivvers" dared tackle the roads around Popham at that time. There was no Mlle Stermaria in the hotel and no Albertine on the beach, but I was much younger than Marcel. Only the two coast guards were firm friends. The hotel guests were only passing figures. I have forgotten their names and faces. But I have not forgotten the excitement I felt in having them about me in the hotel, and in greeting them as Aunt Polly and I walked to our table in the dining room.

I looked forward to each meal, not only because of hunger but because of the novelty of so many dishes, and because of the attractiveness of the young waitresses who served us. There were soups I had never tasted before, and Irish stew at least once a week, fish chowder, bluefish, tongue with boiled potatoes. I learned to enjoy steamed clams. Once—I believe it was only once —my aunt and I were invited to a clambake on the beach where I ate lobster and clams, corn and potatoes, bananas too, and where we drank sarsaparilla. I once tried to count the different kinds of pies that were served for dessert at dinner in the hotel: blueberry, mince, apple, apricot, custard, pumpkin. But my favorite dessert was the chocolate pudding. Much more than the food, the ceremony of eating in a large dining room with other tables close by, and the waitresses coming and going, and a menu held out before me from which I could choose, seemed to me the beginning of a new life. I was awake and excited during the time spent at our table each day. The rest of the time in the hotel I was usually asleep in my bed, and I grew to resent all those hours when I was unconscious and unable to observe the activities and have bits of conversation with this one and that one. I was no longer just a boy, but a wheel of sensations, each turn of which crystallized a moment for me.

There were dramas, too. One morning the fog kept us from taking a small boat to visit one of the lighthouses. I argued with my aunt that the fog would lift, but Aunt Polly never tampered with facts. The fog was there and it was thick. She tried to lessen my disappointment by words, by speaking about the difficulty of living in a lighthouse. I was already somewhat aware that life, in a general way, is difficult, but imagine a lighthouse, imagine being shut up in stormy weather on a rock, with the same waves breaking over it minute after minute. Incapable of untruth, my aunt was one whose kindness was tempered with strictness, and always at such moments of discourse she referred to Mr. Aldrich, superintendent of Brookline schools, for whom she worked. She had to obey him. But I could remember many stories in which he had obeyed her. My coast guards were lenient with me, but not Aunt Polly.

That morning she told me to take my towel, gritty with sand, and shake it outside. The walk to the edge of the water led me through mysterious and almost scary banks of fog. The intoxicating smell of salt and seaweed, and the thought that I might become lost in the fog, turned my mind away from the disappointment of losing out on the trip to the lighthouse. I felt repentant over my silly pleadings with my aunt, and even wondered what ancestral traits of those sluggish Irish and cold Scots might explain my stubbornness.

Cousin Pauline, two years younger than me, joined us on my last summer at Popham, for my second week, and then stayed on longer with our aunt, after I left. She was beautiful, strong, and athletic, surpassing me easily in any physical test. We had grown up together, living in adjoining houses, attending the same schools, having the same teachers. At Popham, Pauline took to South Beach more fervently than I did. There she stayed closer to Aunt Polly's recumbent form than I did. She took delight in collecting shells in the sand and in building sand castles. At low tide she loved the hard wet sand over which she ran and turned cartwheels. Aunt Polly and I would watch her admiringly as she performed one cartwheel after another, her long blonde hair falling this way and that way, her thin light body in constant motion. She did those exercises for her own enjoyment and not at all for us. We watched her turn into a sprite, quite apart from her aunt and cousin, during those exhibition moments of skill. I introduced her to people at the hotel and general store but not to the coast guards. I told her that the board walk was taken up in winter to prevent it being washed out to sea, but I told her very little about the fort in which she showed little interest. The beach was her realm. When it was my turn to go home, and leave my aunt and my cousin, it pleased me to know they would not be invading or enjoying my more secret activities carried out on the top of the fort and in the Coast Guard Station.

3. Le Bois Planté, 1930

These efforts of mine to write out my memoirs and thus record certain happenings and episodes in my life now span a fairly long period of time — more than thirty years. *Pantomime*, the most accurate of my titles for such a book, appeared in 1951. The first and only edition was sold out within three or four years, slowly, because the edition was small. I gave little thought to such writing through the 1960s, but in the seventies a desire to rewrite *Pantomime*, a forgotten book by then, to omit many parts of it and add new parts, was strong enough for me to work on *Journal of Rehearsals*. This appeared in 1977. More attention was paid to it than had been paid to *Pantomime*. *Aubade* was written not because of that attention, but rather because the habit of memoir-writing was part of me then, and the realization that the years ahead for such work, for any work, might be few. It was published in 1983.

Quite honestly I can confess that throughout all of those years, I had planned to write and wanted to write about my second visit to France, in the summer of 1930, following my graduation from Harvard. Each year that I put off this project, I worried that my memory of those two glorious months in the province of Anjou would diminish and blur under the ever-increasing accumulation of so many other memories. My mind was puzzled by this reluctance. Why hadn't I written this episode for *Journal of Rehearsals*, so pervasively concerned with my experiences in France? Why didn't I do it for *Aubade*, in which I placed my visit to the Pyrenees that had taken place long after my first experience with French provincial life when I was twenty-one?

The putting off of this chapter in my life, which I am calling by the mysterious title Le Bois Planté, was due largely to its bigness, to the very difficulty of embracing it and explaining it. I must have dreaded reliving those two months during which I lived the scenes of a novel. It was a family role I played, in a language I had learned in school and in one summer in Paris when I was a tourist taking literature courses and diction lessons. The first summer of 1928 in my *pension de famille* on the rue Léopold-Robert was totally different from my second summer, in a country house on the edge of a vineyard just outside of Angers.

Through a friend in Boston who like myself was planning to be a French teacher, I learned of the Leroy family in Angers. He had lived with them the year before and recommended that I spend part of the summer with them. I wrote to Madame Leroy, at 101, rue du Bellay. The street itself bore the name of the Angevin poet Joachim du Bellay, whose sonnets had taught me something about his province. In my summer course at the Sorbonne in 1928, Monsieur Chamard had read to us many sonnets from *Les Regrets*, and I had memorized the most famous: *Heureux qui comme Ulysse a fait un beau voyage.* When Madame Leroy's answer came inviting me to spend as much of the summer as I wished with her family—her twin sons Maurice and Jean, in their last year at the lycée, and just a few years younger than me—I felt ready to embark on a fine voyage. On purchasing my round-trip boat ticket, I was following the poet's advice to travel and to return home after the glories of the journey ceased to entrance me.

The ghost of Joachim du Bellay hovered over all my preparations for the trip to Angers. His three-year visit to Rome where he worked for his cousin the cardinal in a cardinal's palace, caught up in the fastidious tasks of a high-class housekeeper, paying the huge staff of servants in the *palazzo*, and courting bankers in order to have enough money for such a purpose, turned the excitement of living in the eternal city into the bitterness of exile. With a sense of exaggerated melodrama I compared my insignificant trip to 101, rue du Bellay in 1930, to the Roman journey of du Bellay in the Renaissance, and wondered, with that persistent sense of melodrama, about what *désenchantement* I would encounter in the center of the Leroy family.

The beginning of the summer was to be Paris, a week in the familiar *pension de famille* of Mme Yvet, in Montparnasse. I needed those few days for a rediscovery of what I already knew about France: the streets of Paris, the gardens, the métro, the American Express, le café du Dome, and the bookstore I used on the boulevard Montparnasse. Everything seemed the same as if I had been absent a week rather than two years. My one practical concern was to find the station where I would purchase my train ticket for Angers, and then inform Mme Leroy of the day and hour of my arrival. Then came the more delicate matter of placating Mme Yvet. Only one week at her pension! I assured her that I would spend my last two weeks of the summer with her, in order to relive my Parisian life. The upsurge of her anger lessened, but she was barely placated.

The boat train from Cherbourg to Paris had taken me through Normandy, and the train from Paris to Angers showed me parts of the Ile-de-France and Anjou. I greedily watched that French landscape as it revealed countless details from my readings, such as the slate roofs in Anjou (*l'ardoise fine*, which du Bellay contrasted with *le marbre dur* of Rome), the straight lines of plane trees, *platanes*, the word I had learned in Valéry's poem:

> Tu te penches, grand platane,
> Et te proposes nu!

As I rehearsed these literary reminiscences, the time passed quickly and the train rolled into the station bearing in large clear letters the name: ANGERS. It was the sign of my new life. "Provincial" was the word used to describe that new life long before I had reached this capital city of Anjou, and I was well aware of the slightly demeaning significance it had when used in contrast with its rival term, "Parisian."

I could see them from my train window, the lady and the two young boys, and I inwardly praised the "provincial" attitude, if that was what it was, that brought Mme Leroy and her two sons to greet me at my arrival and accompany me from the station to their home. They were searching for signs of me during the minute or two when I watched them from the *couloir* of my train.

My carefully rehearsed opening sentences were lost in the warm greetings the four of us exchanged. As I was often to experience in France, the speech of the French carried me along and brought forth more spontaneous words and sentiments than those I had planned to use. Mme Leroy was a large woman, with a round smiling face, quite attractive, and she directed our words and gestures as we stood on the *quai*. Maurice, the older boy by two minutes, was dark-haired, and Jean had light hair, almost blond. Both were good-looking and I immediately could distinguish them: Maurice, slightly heavier and more serious-looking; Jean, more affectionate and outgoing, the obvious clown of the family.

They had reserved a taxi. Jean sat with the driver, glad to be separated from the effusions that continued for some time by repetitions. I was soon to learn that when we were together, the Leroys allowed no silence to grow. Thoughts, when they flashed through my mind, had to be expressed orally, and I was to grow skilled in the practice of separating thoughts that might be expressed to the family and thoughts that might be allowed to sink into that silent bottomless subconscious pit where they had been accumulating for twenty years.

Those thoughts that were to be given articulation in my new Angevin life had to be said always in French. This was a new exercise in the expression of thought, more histrionic, more comparable to a stage performance. This new life was to be an adventure which allowed me no time for laziness or indolence. It was also a family adventure, new for an only child accustomed all his life to considerable amounts of solitude and independence.

When the taxi driver asked a question about the exact position of the rue du Bellay, Jean, whose questions were part tease, part joke, asked me whether that name had any meaning for me. Since, after all, I had been a French major at Harvard for four years, I replied (proudly) by quoting: *Heureux qui comme Ulysse a fait un beau voyage*. When the applause subsided, I continued the pedantry by saying that I was here in Anjou for the purpose of understanding what du Bellay meant by *la douceur angevine*. And thus I turned the questions back to Jean and Maurice. Does *douceur* refer to the mildness of the climate or to the gentleness of the inhabitants of Anjou or perhaps to their lethargy? My big question, a retort really to Jean's first question, was, where in French literature does one read about *la douce France*? The boys answered: *La Chanson de Roland*, and we thus started out on an equal footing, evenly provided with classroom clichés.

As I think back now on that distant summer, I see an endless succession of sunlit days, of a family life more indolent than active, of an atmosphere relaxed and friendly, of daily lessons in French where I learned new words both slang and classical, and especially uses of words and expressions, learned without effort, without pain, because I was living within *la douceur angevine*. I wanted more than that *douceur*, whatever it meant, more than the daily immersion in French, more than the novelty of family life where conversation never ceased. I believe I found it, but in so many unobtrusive, unnoticed ways, that only years later, in the fullness of memory, did I realize what I learned, what I absorbed. I lived in constant daily practice of joining my Angevin life with the readings I had done in French books. The language I heard and used that summer was my life.

It stretched out endlessly behind me and before me because, in order to adjust to this mother and her sons, and the grandmother too, whom I met at dinner that first evening, I was using the language —in translation—and the language of Anjou itself. Frequently I was reminded by the Leroys throughout the summer that the speech of Anjou, like that of its neighbor la Touraine, was the purest French, the least affected by traces of dialect, by unusual rhythm and intonation. (Bostonians had often made similar claims about my American accent.) My fate had kept me attached to a region proud of its speech, and had now sent me to a French province that encouraged a comparable pride.

These were the thoughts swirling about in my head the day of my arrival, when I was left alone in my room on the third floor (*au second étage*), with my two bags to be unpacked. The bedroom of Mme Leroy and that of the two boys were on the second floor. Living room, dining room, and kitchen were on the first floor. As I climbed the stairs for the first time, with Maurice who carried one of my bags, I learned that the grandmother lived in the adjoining house with her husband, Monsieur Lemonnier. She spent a good deal of time with her daughter and grandsons because it was she who prepared their lunch and dinner. Monsieur Lemonnier would not be at dinner. He usually ate alone in his own house.

I only partially unpacked because I knew from early correspondence that in a week we would be moving to the country. It was the last week of classes at the lycée. I was too excited to rest, more curious than excited about my arrival in a place I had tried to imagine, and finding myself with people I had tried to imagine. The warm welcome had put me at ease. A totally new life lay ahead of me which would be a more than fitting transition from Harvard to the Taft School and my first full-time post as a French teacher. Cambridge, Anjou, Connecticut. Sites—and also tests. One set of tests and adjustments was over. And this day in early June I was entering upon a second set. The French books I had read at Harvard, those about the provinces in particular—not only Joachim du Bellay, but Ronsard and Montaigne, Barrès and George Sand, Renan and Chateaubriand—they would be my spokesmen now, my initiators and interpreters. I resolved to refrain from literary allusions when talking with my French family. The two worlds of books and daily life were interchangeable for me. One was not more real than the other, and this interchange was more facile in French because of my past four years, and therefore more facile in Anjou.

With that resolution in mind I went down the stairs at seven to meet the grandmother. Doors are kept closed in French houses, and I could hear nothing from the hallway. But on opening the door of the living room, I heard voices and the bustle of dinner preparations. Each of them, the two boys and the two ladies, were making final gestures for dinner: the bottle of wine, the chairs, the soup tureen. Mme Lemonnier was a small lady, gray-haired, smiling unless she pretended to pout or appear insulted by Jean's jibes and hugs. This began with my introduction when Jean said his grandmother wanted to recite du Bellay's sonnet, an allusion she obviously did not remember.

She was the master cook for the family, and her art was very much appreciated. Almost before we exchanged greetings, she announced that she had prepared a special dish in my honor, to welcome me to Angers. There was a bit of a flurry after the soup had been served and eaten. The grandmother came from the kitchen bearing a large platter on which I could see twelve circular objects, green underneath and white on top. The words *coeur d'artichaut* came to my mind instantly. They must be that, but the family had wanted to surprise me with something unknown, untasted. And it was my obligation to express surprise and delight. That moment was another test. Half of the test could be passed because I had never eaten a *coeur d'artichaut* prepared in that way. In Paris two years earlier I had been taught how to nibble the end of each leaf when the entire artichoke was placed before me. To reach and eat the heart was the reward of slow labor *chez* Mme Yvet.

So, I did say, with a question in my voice: *coeurs d'artichauts?* and then immediately said I had never eaten one. Since my knowledge was platonic and linguistic, the grandmother enjoyed my enjoying two *coeurs d'artichaut* with a white sauce (béchamel).

The rest of the dinner continued easily and pleasantly. Maurice took over a bit as head of the family and especially made the point that his mother and grandmother were relieved that I spoke French easily and wanted to understand all the small details that were new to me. I warned him then about my tiresome pedantic traits, about my mind crammed with names of French writers and lines from their works, which I found myself constantly rehearsing when at home as if that act would make France more real to me when I walked along the streets of Boston.

Maurice and the others, on hearing this confession, were puzzled about my being worried that in Angers such references, such recitations would seem out of place. "No, no," he said, "keep rehearsing those facts for our sake. You will remind us of things we should know. But tell me how this has come about."

To answer that question adequately, I would have had to review the last four years of my life, and explain how French words, and the names of French writers had become talismans for me, endowed with magical properties. That was impossible, and so I told the family, as we began eating, at the end of the dinner, our *crème caramel*, about one episode that had occurred at the end of my first visit to France two years earlier.

I explained that by a series of coincidences I was invited to a Sunday lunch at the home of Albert Mockel, the symbolist poet. His name had always been present with those of the more famous symbolists whom I had read. He was so hospitable and gracious, and his wife also, and their other guest, Mme Stuart Merrill, that during the luncheon I plied him with questions about the great writers of his generation. I was greedy to hear about them and dazzled when I did. Back in Paris that night (the Mockels lived in Rueil), I wrote in my journal: "During our conversation I learned that Albert Mockel had seen Verlaine and Rimbaud, had shaken hands with Oscar Wilde, Van Gogh and Gauguin, had said hello to Renoir, had heard Bergson at the Collège de France, and had known Péguy."

Maurice, slightly more than Jean and the two ladies, felt, or knew he should feel, something of the glamour those names held. But he could not have experienced the full excitement that a young American would, who had studied about those figures in America and knew them to be luminaries at the turn of the century, or just before. The name that M. Mockel pronounced with the deepest reverence on that memorable Sunday in Rueil was Stéphane Mallarmé. Most of those men had met one another at Mallarmé's apartment on the rue de Rome and looked upon him, as Mockel did, as the leader, the initiator of them all.

No, Maurice had not heard of Mallarmé, and I resigned myself to the future weeks when I would be discreet and refrain from using such names in this household. They would be weeks of abstinence when I would be the learner and not the teacher. I would learn about the knowledge of Maurice, destined to be a lycée teacher of Greek, and of Jean, destined to be a physician. Their lives were already full of enthusiasms and plans that had no place for fin-de-siècle decadence. Mme Leroy and Mme Lemonnier were more unknowing than the boys of the very select, very limited world of France that I had fashioned for myself. This was my introduction to French provincialism, but I knew it would be erroneous to characterize it as nonliterary. Most of the writers I had just listed, with such obnoxious pedantry, came from provincial cities: Metz, Charleville, Orléans. ·

With the boys in school, and the ladies busy with moving preparations, I spent the days of that first week in Angers walking about the city, and found myself, as the family was also, anxious to move on, anxious to know the relaxed country life I was being promised at every meal.

When France was divided into provinces, Angers was the capital of Anjou. The city just slightly missed being on the Loire River where the famous Renaissance castles are. Angers, on the Maine River, a tributary to the Loire, does not have a Renaissance château, but a feudal castle, with seventeen massive towers. Its history is a rich, confused one of dukes and counts and kings.

The city's pride is in tapestries of the Apocalypse, which on certain feast days are exhibited on the façade of the Cathedral of Saint Maurice. They were invisible those days I explored the city. *Le musée des tapisseries* was closed. I soon learned that Angers is a metropolis, and that the Angevins are more proud of the surroundings than of the city itself, proud of the richness of the soil: vegetables, fruit, flowers (roses and hydrangeas in particular), and vineyards.

The grandfather, a stately and corpulent bearded man, was the lawyer for the Cointreau factory, and he, sensing my slight disappointment with the exterior aspect of Angers, invited me to the factory and distillery, in which I was given a guided tour. That evening after dinner I shared with the family the liqueur I was given in a small sample bottle. Jean carefully explained that Cointreau was too sweet for most men: *c'est une liqueur pour les dames.*

The lycée finally closed its doors, and we set off, the ladies in a hired car with their luggage, and the boys and myself in a train, for the small town at the edge of which we found the property owned by M. Lemonnier, which had been called for generations *Le Bois Planté.* It was a large house, vaguely and modestly resembling a Renaissance château, for indeed we were in the region, as I learned, of many small châteaux, miniature Blois and Amboise. A courtyard came first, large enough for many carriages to drive in at once. On each side of the entrance door to the house were large flowering oleanders—*lauriers roses*—one of the many words from horticulture I had learned in reading French texts and which now I saw in its reality. The main door opened on to a corridor running left and right, and to another door facing it, which opened to a large living room filling the width of the house. Through the French doors straight ahead I could see the vineyard stretching out beyond a small flower garden. I knew I had come to what Anjou was famous for: rich soil for flowers and vineyards.

To the right of the living room were the dining room and kitchen, and to the left two bedrooms on the side of the courtyard for Mme Leroy and Mme Lemonnier. My bedroom was on the ground level also but on the side of the vineyard. The boys' bedroom was upstairs.

A large bed filled most of my room. I could see in a glance that it would serve also as a retreat room, a workroom with a good-sized table close to the window. I made for that immediately, opened it and breathed in the sweet smell of a flower I could not see or name. There were a few rose bushes and hydrangeas, but the smell could not be coming from them. I learned it was jasmine growing obscurely, close to the wall. Just beyond the flower bed and a small path lay the vineyard, rich, immense, beautifully arranged in rows. I was to live this summer practically in a vineyard. I had known of its existence, and wondered why Maurice and Jean had not spoken more often of it or shown more interest in it. Then I remembered there was a *vigneron* who lived with his family close by. That word *vigneron* I knew well, having come across it countless times in Renaissance texts, in Rabelais in particular, but also in works of every century, Zola's *La Terre*, for example, and in Mauriac's novels. I had never found a good translation, a familiar word, for it in English. There were no *vignerons* in New England.

My unpacking took little time, and I soon found myself retracing my steps through the long corridor into the living room and through the French doors into the garden and the vineyard. There was a space close to the house and under a large plane tree for lounging chairs and a table and even a Ping-Pong table. It was an outside salon that we were to use every evening after dinner for relaxation when the conversation would change from the topic of food, a persistent theme during meals, to themes of reminiscences: my childhood in Brookline and the boys' childhood in Angers; World War I, because it was when the boys' father had lost his life; the programs in an American high school and those in a French lycée; a Protestant service and a Catholic mass.

After the first dinner the boys and I came out first and examined the vine plants closest to the house. The small green grapes were already forming. I knew the summer weeks would be measured by their growth. When Mme Leroy came out, she looked at me almost anxiously as if to check on my approval or disapproval of Le Bois Planté. My words reassured her, I think. Then she looked straight across the vineyard to the horizon against which stood out one solitary rather scrubby-looking tree. At such a distance I could make out only angular branches. "My favorite tree," she said. "I look at it every evening after dinner to see if it is still there. If it is there, I know we are here too, and all is well."

I asked her what kind of tree it was, and she answered a bit surprised, "I think it is a *cormier*, but I have never been sure." That was a new word for me — *cormier* — and that night in my room I looked for it in a small pocket dictionary I carried with me. But there was no *cormier*. We referred to the *cormier* so often that summer that the tree and the word representing it became fixed in my mind in the same way. Maurice and Jean had learned it from their mother when they were very young. Much later, back home in Brookline, with my dictionaries I learned that *cormier* was a regional word, a vulgar Latin word in fact, for *sorbier*, which in English means "a service-tree." An Old World tree of which the reddish fruit is eaten by birds. That summer I did see the red fruit and watched flocks of birds fighting over the berries. Then one day, years later, I read in a Nerval story the phrase: *sorbiers à grains de corail*. "Coral" was indeed the color of the berries. Literature came at last to crown one of my language lessons in Anjou.

The grandfather came on the first weekend. Actually he arrived late Saturday, after dinner, and left Sunday afternoon. His presence made Sunday lunch an event, and it was during that meal that I had my first chance to see him closely and even to talk with him. He was the father figure of the family: corpulent, bearded, aware of his position of responsibility, listened to with respect, gruff in his answers, as taciturn as the two ladies were loquacious. I felt awe when from time to time he addressed a question to me. The boys seemed to feel both awe and pride. I had questions for him which I never asked: why didn't he join the family at dinners in Angers? why did he eat alone in his own house, as I was informed he did? why did he spend only twenty-four hours a week at Le Bois Planté? why did he refrain from joining in the general conversation? I had to make up answers to these questions, and by the middle of the summer I had decided that the talk of his daughter and wife, and the chatter too of his grandsons, wearied him. They were anxious to involve him, and he was determined to avoid any involvement with words and emotions. His silence was his strength, and the sign of his authority.

I had been told that the principal course for Sunday lunch was—inevitably —a *poulet rôti*, and it was as large a chicken as I have ever seen, roasted to perfection, and lauded by all of us when Jean carried it to the table, followed by his grandmother who unexpectedly appeared charmingly modest in not wishing to hear the praise for her cookery skill. Before the chicken reached the table, with its well-deserved fanfare, while we were still eating our *tomate vinaigrette*, I sensed that some other ritual was being made ready for which I had not been prepared. Monsieur Lemonnier initiated the mystery when he said to the boys: "It is time to go downstairs and choose the wine."

La cave was the word he used, and it was at that time the only part of the house I had not been shown. Maurice winked at me and Jean smiled knowingly. They disappeared but were back in just a few minutes. Maurice came to me with the bottle of wine. During their absence the grandfather explained to me that all the wine they drank at Le Bois Planté was from their own vineyard. In the *cave* there was good and less good wine, and for Sunday lunch he always insisted that his grandsons choose the wine from one of the good years.

On the label on the bottle that Maurice showed me I saw the year 1922 and the words *côté nord*. He directed me to say nothing, and then opened the bottle, poured half a glass, and handed the glass to his grandfather. I realized by this time that they were testing their grandfather. He tasted the wine, held it in his mouth a few seconds, swallowed, and then—it was the first time I had seen him smile—said in his usual laconic style: "1922, côté nord."

This ritual was enacted every Sunday, when I tasted a white wine superior to any *vin blanc* I have tasted since that time. Not once did M. Lemonnier fail his test—and there was quite a span of years, and some years the *côté sud* had produced a finer wine than the *côté nord*. The ladies never drank any wine. Only the men at the table indulged, and after his first glass the grandfather usually favored me with a few words.

That first Sunday, for example, he asked me if I planned to take any short trips in Anjou since there were many easily accessible places. He mentioned Saumur, famous for its cavalry school, for Balzac, and for its white wine. I had not even considered such expeditions. The ladies disapproved immediately, and said so. "He is here to practice French and not to travel," they said, and rejected the grandfather's words: "He will be bored if he stays here all summer."

I had been reading—almost surreptitiously—a small guidebook of Anjou I had found on the one shelf of books in Le Bois Planté. The grandfather's words encouraged me to consider at least one trip in order to break—as he would have said—the monotony of my summer existence. Actually it was not monotonous for me, but the same pedantic drive in me to learn from the daily speech I engaged in also urged me to add to my scanty knowledge of France. One page in the guidebook attracted me more than all the others. It was the description of the small town of Sablé-sur-Sarthe with its Benedictine Abbey of Solesmes. I had become interested in Gregorian music, or plainchant, used by the Cowley Fathers in Cambridge in their Anglican monastery, and in their parish church of St. John the Evangelist in Boston. But I had rarely heard plainchant sung in Latin, as it should be. Solesmes was world-famous at that time for the medieval authenticity of its song.

I determined to make at least that one trip to the Benedictines, and with foreknowledge that there would be objections from the family, I began hinting at the trip strategically from time to time. Even the boys, whom I counted on being more broad-minded than the ladies, hesitated to back me up. They had become used to my presence. We had begun talking together more frequently and more frankly. They called themselves my *professeurs d'argot*, teachers of the slang words and phrases I began assigning to a special notebook.

Maurice, who always seemed older than Jean, although it was only by a few minutes according to Mme Leroy, was the most understanding of my habits of study and even of my perverse desire to visit Solesmes. And he did check for me the means by which I could reach Sablé. It would mean the short train ride to Angers, and then a bus to Sablé. I looked about then for some convincing reasons that would justify my desertion, and found it in a liturgical phrase I began hearing—a coming feast day: *La Fête-Dieu*. Mme Leroy and the boys regularly attended mass. The grandparents seemed not to practice their religion. When one evening at dinner Maurice asked me what Americans call *La Fête-Dieu*, I replied, "Corpus Christi," and added, spontaneously, "I have decided to make the trip to Solesmes for *La Fête-Dieu*, to see the procession and to hear high mass sung in plainchant."

It was a master stroke. Mme Leroy seemed even a bit envious. Mme Lemonnier begrudgingly said her husband would approve. The boys began giving me advice of a practical nature. I would go the next Wednesday and spend two nights in Sablé, allowing me to follow the vigil service on Wednesday, the procession and mass on Thursday, and Compline on Thursday night.

In the few remaining days I deliberately refrained from any mention of Solesmes, and the family also was mute, but I sensed that their fundamental disapproval had begun to grow again. Their silence on the subject was a verdict and a punishment. The grandfather who would have supported me was far away in Angers.

One incident helped out. The morning after a heavy rainfall one night, the boys and I were wandering about the garden and the vineyard. They began noticing a large number of snails appearing everywhere, especially on the privet bushes. Jean left us to consult with his grandmother, and returned, his face beaming. "Yes, she will cook them." I was then initiated into the collecting of snails and the elaborate process of preparing them to be eaten.

Each of us had a bucket, reserved for this purpose, into which we placed the snails. It was an easy hunt: they were plentiful. The buckets were then placed in the cellar, covered for three days in order to starve the snails. Then they would be fed white flour for three more days, at the end of which they would be cooked. By then I would be back from Solesmes, and I would eat snails for the first time in my life. This meal would fall on the Sunday after Corpus Christi. Monsieur Lemonnier would be present.

Nothing had really been forgiven, but an atmosphere of resignation reigned, and an absence of any enthusiasm that would bolster my own growing enthusiasm. So I left Le Bois Planté alone, that Wednesday. My walk to the station was a bit sad, but the sadness evaporated as I continued the journey on that sunny June day. I can remember no hitch in the travel plans Maurice had worked out for me. I reached Sablé, found a room in a hotel, and made my way to the monastery along the Sarthe River.

There were a few other visitors like myself and each of us was assigned a guide, a brother of the order. I was given to Frère Joseph, a most amiable fellow about my own age, I would guess, who showed me a few parts of the monastery first before taking me to the church. The guidebook I had consulted at Le Bois Planté served me when I asked about the earliest part of the priory, founded in the eleventh century. Frère Joseph forthwith led me to the crypt and pointed out parts of the foundation believed to be of the eleventh century. But there were many changes when the priory was made an abbey in 1835 by Gregory XVI. I asked if that was when plainchant was rediscovered and sung by the monks. "Not until the end of the century," was the reply. "You see, it is quite recent, and yet it is already so well-known. Where do you come from?"

When I explained that I had just finished my undergraduate studies at Harvard, he informed me with some degree of pride: "Yes, we have had musicians from Harvard, and from other institutions near Harvard, who have spent days, weeks here listening to the singing of the hours, and discussing musical matters with a few of the fathers who direct the singing, who train us." In the church he pointed out the place for visitors and suggested that I return at eight for the preliminary vigil service and stay on at nine for Compline, the last sung hour of the day. On Sunday the procession was to begin at ten and end with high mass at eleven. I was welcome to join the procession with other visitors and enter the church with them at the end of the procession.

He asked only one technical question. "Do you understand that the Blessed Sacrament is in the monstrance, held by the priest who walks in the center of the procession?" I told him I did understand, but refrained from pointing out that I had learned it from an Anglican order in Cambridge, Massachusetts.

Only some of the monks sang the two offices I followed that evening in the church. I was deeply moved by the chanting, by the modulation of the voices that seemed to be one voice. Two lines of the Latin that were repeated often came clear to me. The syllables were so distinct that I could join silently with them:

> Lauda Sion salvatorem!
> Lauda ducem et pastorem!

It was indeed praise of God in song. The words were held in the air and then dissolved into other words.

I walked back to the hotel with a few of the visitors and learned from them that I might have stayed at the monastery had I written early for a reservation. A quietness had settled over the town as if it were a prolongation of Solesmes. After the last notes of Compline had been sung, the monks entered the greater silence that would last until the first notes of Prime in early morning.

In the silence of my own room, my thoughts were very much fixed on the mystery of the monastic vocation I had observed in the cloisters of the abbey and in the church during the chanting of Compline. It was a mystery: the resolution of a soul to live according to the ancient rule of Saint Benedict. These men lived in the midst of the world, in the town of Sablé in Anjou, and yet they were cut off from the world. From all I had observed during those first few hours, they were living in a joyous apostolate. I wondered about what had made them decide to become Benedictines rather than Carthusians, or Franciscans, or Trappists, or Dominicans, or Jesuits. Why had they chosen the black habit of Saint Benedict rather than the white-collared habit of Saint Dominic? They lived and worked a thousand years away from twentieth-century France in their medieval clothes and diet and Gregorian chant. Did they suffer from the claustrophobia of the enclosed life?

The great bell tolled at five in the morning. I was told that on feast days Prime and Matins were sung together at six o'clock. I was in the church in time to watch the monks file into their stalls. The greater silence was broken then by the singing of the first prayers and psalms of the day. It would be a public day of rejoicing, with many visitors who had come to watch and listen and pay their devotion to the Blessed Sacrament, on the *Fête-Dieu* of that year of 1930.

Only two or three visitors were with me at that first hour. They were there, as I was, to enjoy the simplicity and beauty that marked everything the Benedictines did in their liturgy. The sun was rising, and soon the church was full of light. The monks stood in their stalls and at the end of each psalm bowed their heads low. They seemed to me to be hidden in the anonymity of their choir and their cowls. The many side altars lining the nave were occupied by monks saying their private masses. What an unending, unchanging spectacle the liturgy is! Just a few hours ago I had followed the night office. Now with the new day all was beginning again.

I returned to the hotel for breakfast, but was soon back in order to watch the forming of the procession and to take my own place in it, among the visitors. The little girls of the town were the most excited. They were dressed in white and carrying small wicker baskets of rose petals. They were placed immediately in front of the celebrant, the priest carrying the large gold monstrance with the Sacrament, the Corpus Christi, in the center under glass. The girls would scatter the rose petals at the feet of the celebrant during the procession.

As we were taking our places, I asked one of the visitors if the procession would go through part of the town. He said no. It would simply move around the buildings of the monastery and the church. He concluded his explanation with a sentence that awakened in me rich literary memories that had been striving to surface every since I had reached Solesmes. *Il n'y aura pas de reposoirs.* (There will be no altars of repose.)

Reposoir was a word I had first learned in Flaubert's *Un coeur simple.* The *Fête-Dieu* procession is the ceremony filling the last page of the story. Félicité dies at the moment when the outside procession passes under her window when she can smell the incense and see in her mind the monstrance as the priest blesses the crowd from the improvised altar of repose, on which Loulou, the stuffed bedraggled parrot, was half hidden under flowers. The three French words ending in -*oir*, forming a rhyme in Flaubert's prose — *reposoir, encensoir* (censer), and *ostensoir* (monstrance)—are used as legitimate rhymes in Baudelaire's poem *Harmonie du soir.*

The trio of words revived my memory and resounded in my mind as I quite literally lived them during the Solesmes procession. From my place near the end of the line, I could see the monstrance far ahead of me as it was held high above the head of the celebrant. It was indeed a golden rival of the sun. I could hear the clanging of the censers manipulated by young boys, who shot out streams of incense every few minutes when they turned and directed the incense toward the monstrance. At the climax of the procession, when we were all in the church, filling it to its limits, the celebrant-priest slowly mounted the steps to stand before the high altar. He turned then, and, facing us all, blessed us by making the sign of the cross with the monstrance.

By that time I had become accustomed to the slowness and dignity of the Benedictines in their somber habits. The monstrance was placed on a stand above the high altar, and everything was cleared away for the beginning of the mass itself. The cope was removed from the shoulders of the monk who had carried the monstrance in the procession, and placed on a very tall monk who was to celebrate the mass after he sprinkled the congregation with holy water. It was the *Asperges me.* The splendor of the ceremony and the fervor of the monks—those serving at the altar as deacon and subdeacon, and those in their stalls singing the plainchant according to the ancient rites of Saint Benedict—restored for me on that morning at Solesmes the freshness of the earliest Christian mysteries. Slowly and with absolute assurance, the monks moved toward the moment when the large white Host was raised and when the chalice of Our Lord was raised high in the hands of the celebrant. When the bell of the elevation was rung, I was emptied of everything extraneous and trivial. I was ready to receive the Idea of God, and then the Corpus Christi.

At that time in my life I had no way of knowing that ahead of me I was to know three other moments of a comparable religious experience in the presence of the reserved Sacrament: the plainsong of the Benedictine Sisters on the rue Monsieur in Paris, the tiny chapel of Jacques and Raïssa Maritain in their house at Meudon where by some exceptional permission from Rome the Sacrament was reserved permanently, and the singing of the Benedictines at Saint-Benoît-du-Lac outside of Montreal where the leaders singing in the choir had been trained at Solesmes.

That first experience of the *Fête-Dieu* stayed with me during the following days at Le Bois Planté—but it was unspoken. It took some time for me to be reinstated in the Leroy family. Their irritability was expressed only in not asking me any questions about Solesmes. But even that changed in time, and gradually when it was certain I was planning no more flights, the questions were asked, by the grandfather first, and then by Maurice and Jean. The prodigal was back. The Sunday chicken was roasted. The bottle of white wine from some auspicious year was opened.

I was more than willing to resume interest in food and cookery. That began a few days after my return, with the snails. They had been fattened on white flour: plump and delicious they were, but more than the snails themselves I enjoyed *la farce*, the filling at the mouth of the shell, with its strong taste of garlic and butter.

When the topic of snails was exhausted, the boys took me one afternoon in the small boat on the pond, and we fished, not for the carp that lived in the pond, but for frogs. On the hooks of our fish lines we placed patches of red cloth and dangled them over the surface close to the edge of the pond. The frogs leapt out of the water and hooked themselves on the disguised hooks. They seemed decidedly repulsive to me, and my catch was negligible. However I did eat for dinner that evening *cuisses de grenouille*.

Every few days I would walk alone up and down the rows of vine plants and check the growth of the grapes on the vines. Thus I measured the passing days and weeks. My existence was hopelessly undramatic. I felt some physical tiredness because much of our activity was outside. But I felt also a too slight activity of the brain. I worked each morning on some writing, and whenever a piece of it was finished, a sense of relief as well as a sense of disappointment would settle over me. As the grapes enlarged on the vine plants, so did my thoughts about the final days in Paris, during which I felt certain of recapturing the excitement of a city, both its beauty and the intellectual stimulus I needed. My French family life was drawing to a close. It had been warm and rewarding with just a few moments of tension that inevitably characterize family life. I had feared—unconsciously—becoming too attached, because even then, at the early age of twenty, I lived in dread of sentimentality.

My actual departure at the train in Angers was tearful. The only member of the family absent from that scene was the grandfather. He was probably the one who understood me the best, who willingly granted me that degree of freedom on which I relied for physical release and independence of spirit.

Memories of Le Bois Planté come back to me fifty years later, largely because of words I learned and heard there as they were used in daily speech: Mme Leroy's favorite tree, *le cormier*, and her expression, *"Jean déraille"*— inevitably used when Jean told a story and became confused over details. I had not heard that phrase before, but I knew *le rail* and realized she was saying "Jean is off the track." Good-naturedly Jean accepted his mother's verdict, and she eased his feelings with the phrase, said really to herself: *mon petit gars. Gars* too was a new word (from *garçon*) and pronounced without the sound of the *r*. I often visited a farmer nearby. I was the first American he had met, and on each of my visits he would ask the same question: *Est-ce qu'on prie le bon Dieu là-bas comme ici?* It was hard for him to realize that at such a distance from France, prayers might be directed to the same God. On the way back from his house I collected blackberries that were plentiful along the roadside. After teaching me the words *mûres sauvages*, all the family expressed consternation over my desire to eat them (with a little milk) for dessert. Not one of them would consent to tasting *les mûres*. This act of mine broke all the rules for eating at Le Bois Planté. It was a more minor gaffe than Solesmes, but it took a few days for the infraction to be forgiven, although not forgotten.

Mme Yvet's *pension de famille* in Paris was a totally different atmosphere. The table was always crowded at dinner, and there was no discussion of the food we consumed greedily. We narrated in our various French accents things we had done or seen that day. A family scene, in a way, but without any possessive factors. Mme Yvet was interested in a few of us, and less interested in the others. She had seen so many come and go, from so many different countries. Through the years she had learned to practice the art of discretion. Each of us at table revealed what he wanted to, and Mme Yvet never pried. She encouraged conversation but on universal topics: Paris, monuments in the capital, new and old French literature, history, politics, the theater. Each of us lived publicly in his own private world. My room at the pension was comfortable, the meals were more than satisfactory, the company was almost members of a classroom where we ate our *artichauts* or our *purée de pomme de terre*, where we recited and learned words, phrases, bits of information.

At the first dinner on my return from Angers, an English lady who worked in the Paris office of the *Daily Mail*, told me that Picasso was always visible in Le Select at the aperitif hour before lunch. The next day when I began my planned and desired renewed explorations of the city, I walked by La Rotonde, close by on the Boulevard Montparnasse, and then, just a bit farther on, stopped at the entrance to Le Select. There in the back of the café, in the midst of friends, Pablo Picasso reigned at a large table. In 1930 he was well-known but not yet world-famous. I was never to see him again at that close distance. A few of the waiters eyed me suspiciously. I would have to sit down at a table or move on. I moved on, crossed the boulevard, passed La Coupole and Le Dôme on my way back to the rue Léopold-Robert and my lunch at Mme Yvet's.

That momentary sight of Picasso, holding forth vociferously with friends at Le Select, reinitiated me into the world I loved and from which I had been absent many weeks. I would have only a few days in Paris—about ten— before taking the boat back to New York and to my first full-time teaching post at Taft School in Connecticut. Every walk I took in Paris those last days of the summer was somehow related to French literature, and whatever conversation I had and whatever note-taking I took, were related to the French language which I was to teach in a week or two in my first official capacity.

The decade of the 1920s had come to an end, and little did I realize at that time how rich those years were in both American and French culture: the Chaplin films I had seen, Stravinsky's music I had heard with the Boston Symphony, Pablo Picasso whom now I had seen in the flesh in a Paris café. The 1930s had just opened, and somehow I felt as I looked ahead that the future was not so gaily colored. Hemingway was the best-known of the new American novelists, and he was living in Paris. I had just read *A Farewell to Arms* (1929), a definitive book on the last war that had ended when I was ten. Before that we had all read *The Sun Also Rises* of 1926. But a book preceding those two, *The Great Gatsby* (1925) by F. Scott Fitzgerald, had seemed to be *the* book on the jazz age. And Fitzgerald too was associated with Paris.

I spent the morning of my first full day in Paris in the vicinity of la rue de l'Odéon where I wanted to see the two bookstores, monuments to literature-in-the-making, for Americans and French alike. At number 7, rue de l'Odéon I found *Les amis des livres*, and knew it to be the bookstore of Adrienne Monnier, where André Gide often came, and Léon Paul Fargue. I knew it to be an active center of modern literature, but did not know, of course, that it would continue to be so until the middle of the century.

Opposite *Les amis des livres*, I found the equally famous bookstore, Shakespeare and Company, founded by Sylvia Beach, a good friend of Adrienne

Monnier. There the display of modern English and American books pulled me back into my orbit. A prominent place was given to a single copy of *Ulysses*. I asked about the price of the blue-covered volume, and was told it was the last copy they had of the first edition, and it was not for sale. If I returned in a few days there would be copies of a new edition. On certain evenings Shakespeare and Company was converted into a literary salon where English, American, and French writers met and talked in the very place where their books were sold. I had read the list several times: Ezra Pound and T. S. Eliot, Scott Fitzgerald and Ernest Hemingway. French literature was well represented by Paul Valéry, Jules Romains, and Valery Larbaud.

I was in the midst of a historical period which, fifteen years later, was to be called *l'entre-deux-guerres*. Those last days of August 1930 were sunlit and peaceful as I made my rounds in memory of writers and artists who had made Paris their center, for at least part of their lives. On one of my walks I stood before number 27, rue de Fleurus, and thought of Gertrude Stein and wondered if she were at home. Her salon of avant-garde painting and literature had preceded and followed World War I, and I rehearsed the names of those she had spoken of and even promoted: Guillaume Apollinaire, who had died in Paris on the day of the Armistice 1918; and the two good friends of Apollinaire who used to come down from Montmartre to visit Gertrude Stein: Max Jacob and Pablo Picasso. She was mentor for Hemingway, promoter of Matisse, friend of André Salmon and Jean Cocteau.

I walked through the streets of Paris, and at the same time I reviewed what I knew—so sketchily—of the twenties, the decade when I had been a high school and college student. The year of 1922 was in my mind, my freshman year in Brookline High School, when events took place of which I was at that time unaware: the publication of Eliot's "The Waste Land," the publication of Joyce's *Ulysses* here in Paris, the death of Marcel Proust. Then I shifted my attention, in this historical survey, to the year 1925–26, my senior year and the year also of the first cantos of Ezra Pound, *The Great Gatsby*, the founding of the *New Yorker*, Chaplin's *The Gold Rush*, André Gide's *Les Faux-Monnayeurs*.

Throughout my college years, 1926–30, I had read several books by Gide, and reread them for their message, their style, their humanity. At that moment in my life I knew the writings of Gide better than those of any other French writer. In memory of the opening pages of his autobiography, *Si le grain ne meurt*, I took the rue Vavin on my second morning to the Luxembourg, crossed the garden to the rue de Médicis, number 19, where Gide was born and where he lived the first five years of his life. I looked up at the balconies of that house without knowing which one had belonged to his father's apartment, and from which paper dragons fashioned by his father were launched through the air to the pond on the square and even to the garden itself.

Nearby on the rue de Tournon, I stopped briefly at number 2, where the Gide family lived for the following seven years, a house in which Balzac had once lived. Gide had written especially of his father's study in that apartment, with its books and papers, and of the veneration he had felt for his father's knowledge. This particular section of Paris, the fourteenth and sixth *arondisse-ments*, was the first I grew to know fairly well. The *carrefour*, or intersection of two boulevards, Montparnasse and Raspail, and the rue Vavin, was my center, close to my pension, and close to the three cafés I passed so often: Le Dôme, la Rotonde, and la Coupole, celebrated by Hemingway in *The Sun Also Rises*, and celebrated in the thirties by Henry Miller in *The Tropic of Cancer*.

After my Gidian walk to the rue de Tournon, and from then on during my last days of August, I was seized with a fever to see all, in a pedantic review of French literature and of streets I had known in the summer of 1928. On the small street Campagne 1ère, parallel to Léopold-Robert, I went into the res-taurant which the proprietor had told me Modigliani frequented, not for food, but for glasses of white wine which he paid for with a few canvases. On return trips from greater distances, I stopped always for a quiet moment on la Place Saint-Sulpice, where I sat on a bench facing the awesome façade of the church, with its memory for me of Balzac's *La messe de l'athée*, and looked at the foun-tain with its four statues of bishops: the famous ones of Bossuet and Fénelon, and the less famous Fléchier and Massillon. I looked at the building which was once *le séminaire de Saint-Sulpice*, where Ernest Renan studied to become a priest and where he lost his faith. It was there that Des Grieux, a fictional seminarian, received the visit of Manon, in Prévost's novel.

A veritable literary pilgrimage those last days, those last hours became, when greed and giddiness grew in me. At the pension dinners, I rehearsed what I had seen. I turned each dinner into a survey course on French literature, and Mme Yvet relaxed from her usual role of questioner and director of the conversation. In my Harvard course on Symbolism, my professor had not found time to study with us the poems of Mallarmé (we all felt he was not quite ready to tackle those poems), but I had tried to read some on my own, and I knew of 89, rue de Rome, near the Gare St. Lazare. That address I visited for the first time and saw the plaque at the entrance telling all literary tourists like myself that Stéphane Mallarmé had lived in that building on the *quatrième étage*, between 1871 and 1898. It was the site of the *mardis soirs*, the gatherings of writers and painters. I had no notion at that time, only perhaps the vaguest premonition, that Mallarmé was eventually to take over a large part of my life.

The Saint-Germain section of Paris was not in 1930 as famous for literature as it was to be by the end of the decade and throughout the forties. Largely because of Apollinaire, whose poems I was beginning to read, I stopped in front of 202, boulevard Saint Germain, where he lived for six years before his death in 1918. Le café de Flore and le café des Deux Magots were crowded on the late afternoons I walked past them, not to observe them so much as to observe la Brasserie Lipp on the opposite side of the boulevard, and to sit for a moment inside the church of Saint-Germain-des-Prés.

Near the Panthéon, in the Latin Quarter, I went to the church of Saint Etienne-du-Mont, to pass by the golden or gilded tomb of Sainte Geneviève, but especially to pass by the two plaques indicating the graves of Pascal and Racine. I remembered too that the funeral service of Verlaine was held in that church. I ended these visits with a slow return to the rue de Médicis and the rue de Tournon in memory of Gide's *Si le grain ne meurt*. That summer I had bought the current available edition. The book was first published in 1925–26, still another literary work of that rich central year of the decade. I had read the night before my last day the pages in the early part of the book on Miss Anna Shackleton, the unmarried woman whose origin was Scotland, and who had been first governess of Gide's mother, and then governess of young André himself.

The passage was one to which I had returned many times. The skill, the deftness of Gide the writer is on those pages, but also the heart of Gide is revealed there in the sympathy he felt for another human being. Without a family of her own, Anna Shackleton became a member of Gide's family. A full human figure is depicted in just a few lines: her poverty, the modesty of her character, her kindness, the embroidery that occupied all her spare moments, her skill in languages—English, French, German, Italian—her serious study of botany, and her role as Gide's teacher of botany, which was to become an important occupation throughout his life.

Anna lived in a small apartment on the rue de Vaugirard between the rue Madame and the rue d'Assas. I went to that spot my last day in Paris, but did not know the exact building in which she had lived. When André Gide began attending the Ecole Alsacienne, he was allowed to stop at Anna's home for lunch one day a week. Each of those visits was meaningful because of the strong affection that joined them. A loving indulgence surrounded the meal. Gide recorded an exclamation he made at the beginning of one of the lunches, which caused him to blush with embarrassment then and whenever he thought of it afterward: "Anna, je vais te ruiner!" It implied, of course, unconsciously, a reference to her poverty.

In a curious way—but perhaps not so curious—the story of Anna Shackleton in Gide's family bore a resemblance to my own role in the Leroy family at Le Bois Planté. Memories of those sunny days spent close to the vineyard grew into memories of happiness as I joined them with the renewed memories of Paris and of French writers. In both places, in Anjou and in the streets of the capital, I stalked experiences that were slight and fugitive and even pedantic in one sense, but which in their accumulation formed the basis of a large part of my life that was still to be lived.

4. Sever Hall

During the eight years I studied at Harvard—four years as undergraduate, and four years as graduate student and instructor in French—Sever Hall, in the center of the Yard, close to Widener Library and Memorial Chapel, was the building where I spent most of the classroom hours, either listening to my professors or teaching the freshmen, five or six years younger than myself. On the second floor there is a classroom containing only four or five rows of benches with ten or twelve seats each, and facing a slightly elevated platform with the teacher's desk, a comfortable chair, and a podium that might be placed on the desk if the teacher chose to stand.

In my junior year I enrolled in an advanced course in French conversation conducted by Professor Louis Mercier, a most amiable man well-known for his two leading interests: the teaching of French, a late-afternoon graduate course taken by high school French teachers in the Boston area; and "humanism," as expounded by Irving Babbitt. At the same time I was taking Babbitt's course on Rousseau and romanticism and soon heard in Mercier's remarks echoes of Babbitt's philosophy concerning morality and literature. To distinguish the Harvard-Babbitt system from Renaissance humanism, Mercier used the term *l'humanisme américain*, and in fact gave that title to his book which appeared a few years later.

The classroom in Sever was the site all year long of the Mercier course. It was also the classroom where in 1933 I listened to T. S. Eliot explain to a group of students who the important contemporary writers were, especially Yeats,

Joyce, Conrad, Pound, D. H. Lawrence, and Henry James. Eliot gave the
Charles Eliot Norton public lectures that year, and the contract called for his
teaching a small class as well. The same classroom was assigned to me a few
years later for one of my sections when I taught a course entitled, "Readings in
French literature."

There were approximately fifteen students in the Mercier course and in the
Eliot course, as well as in the classes where I was instructor. Professor Mercier's attitude toward all of us was fatherly. Mr. Eliot was more reserved, more
distant. His talks were largely anecdotal. Our work in the Mercier course
consisted in preparing and giving each week a short talk in French on a topic of
our choice. Thus we learned quite a bit about one another. Some of the fellows
had grown up in France, others had lived there for long periods of time, and all
were attached in some way or other to France and proud of speaking fluently.

Equality reigned in that class as it reigned in no other class I ever attended or
taught. A few of us enjoyed making our little speeches more than the others.
That was the only difference I sensed. All of us wanted some practice in
speaking French, and a few were lazy about carrying out the desire. Professor
Mercier's ruddy face smiled whenever one of us made a mistake in the gender
of a noun or in the use of a verb tense or in the accent of an unusual word. The
questions he asked at the end of each speech were not about the content or the
style of the speech, but they tried to maneuver us in the direction of thoughts
that preoccupied him at that point in his life. Early in the course we became
aware of those thoughts: the relationship between literature and life; the difference between romanticism and classicism; the Aristotelian code of ethics.
Thoughts not at all unlike those articulated a few years later, in the same
classroom, by T. S. Eliot.

Professor Mercier spoke French slowly. He never seemed to me a Frenchman speaking. On Sunday afternoons he received students for tea. I went a few
times and met his wife and a few of their many children. The Merciers,
passionately devoted to France, seldom went there. They had adopted American life—Cambridge and Boston life—and their children were decidedly
American. Professor Mercier's profession was the teaching of the French language to French teachers, and the teaching of French thought, customs, and
history to the group of students he had every year in advanced French conversation. In class I always worried when a student asked him to translate a word
he had forgotten or had never known. At times there were prolonged embarrassing waits for the French word, and at times no word was forthcoming, or
we heard a weak phrase for a substitution. We gradually learned not to ask and
simply used the English word as if the French equivalent did not exist.

It was my easiest course because I had always been able to memorize quickly. And I rather enjoyed sitting in a chair on the platform close to Professor Mercier's chair-behind-the-desk. It was for me more a course in histrionics than a course in French. In the sixth grade in the Edward Devotion School in Brookline we were trained to give "oral themes." They were my most successful grammar school exercises, and there in Sever Hall I was giving the same — almost the same — speeches in French. My goal was not so much to please Professor Mercier as to hold the attention of my fellow students.

When not giving my speech, I sat in the middle of the second row. The few seats in row one near the door were kept for those students who arrived late, even later than Professor Mercier. The rest of us kept our same seats and talked with one another before the class began. Paul Schofield, from Chicago, always arrived a few minutes after me and took the seat to my right. I enjoyed his conversation as well as his speeches. Quite early in the course a tone of mutual confidence and friendship was established, and it grew steadily throughout the year and the years afterward. Paul was my opposite in most ways: more worldly than I was, more witty, more self-assured, more familiar with French provinces — I had spent the entire summer just in Paris — and much more familiar with the contemporary literary scene in America.

It became a game with us to surprise the other with our speech of the week. But it was not easy to surprise, or better, to shock Paul. He prodded me into trying to dazzle or even daze him. *Etonne-moi!* (We knew the famous command Diaghilev had given Cocteau.) Now, exactly fifty-five years later, I have no memory of what topics I spoke on, although I remember that my best oral theme in the sixth grade was on the sinking of the *Lusitania*. Not a scrap of paper has been preserved that might give me a clue. I suppose all those words, all those sentences have gone into subsequent talks I have given — like the exercises of a runner or of a basketball player, where nothing is remembered except the marathon or the game. Exposed to the fierce light of publicity, I wanted each speech to be better than the ones already given. In this I was motivated more by the jaunty words and attentiveness of Paul than by the comments of Professor Mercier.

Paul accused me of giving "highbrow" talks, unduly egotistical. By that, I presumed he meant all my references were to French literature or to the customs of the French I had observed in my Paris summer. He was more cosmopolitan than I was and made references to American and English literature as often as to French. I admired the breadth of his mind and interests, and felt too exclusively Gallic as we chatted side by side. Our friendship during the first two months of the course grew there in row two of the Sever classroom.

Then one day, just before the class began, he leaned over close to me as if his question was to be secret and private: "Have you read any T. S. Eliot yet?" When I said, "No," he pantomimed a shocked expression, saying: "You better get with it, champ, he's the biggest thing with the English majors, at least with the elitist Harvard boys."

From Paul I first learned the name of T. S. Eliot. That very day, after class, I bought two books at the Coop, a volume of poems and one of essays. What revelations they were ("Aunt Helen" and "*The Boston Evening Transcript*") and were to be ("Prufrock" and "The Waste Land"). And there was an essay on Babbitt, whose course I was taking and also hearing about in a somewhat unusual form in the French conversation course. So Paul and I talked in row two about Eliot, and then continued talking about him in Paul's room in Massachusetts Hall. Paul encouraged me to use his room as often as I wished. At that time I was teaching two French classes at Rivers School in Brookline and tutoring a few high school pupils. So I lived in Brookline and bought my first car, a light brown Ford which allowed me to be student and teacher: a dual life-style that continued to the moment as I write these sentences.

I basked in Paul's friendship and hospitality. I met his mother, a fine painter and a disciple of Survage. To be close to her master, she spent a large part of each year in southern France. Both she and Paul preferred to live away from Chicago, the site of their permanent home. I spent so many evenings in Massachusetts Hall that I felt as if Paul's rooms were mine too. He rode his mind at a gallop in pursuit of an idea. I argued with him about the need to be a "highbrow." Wasn't Flaubert one? and Racine? and Proust? and Keats dying of consumption at the age of twenty-six?

After such a list, Paul countered with: "Highbrows don't deal with real life!" When I then used the name of Eliot, I pleased him by saying: "Eliot has shown me what my life looks like. He has helped show me what I have to do to make something out of my life."

Paul had no desire to be a teacher, but he did want to be a writer. That was our great bond, I suppose. The example of Eliot's fame inspired him more than Eliot's writings. Paul revealed for me a relationship between the self I knew and the world outside of myself. He literally helped me to connect with the world outside. He savored the words in a poem more than I did at that time. He kept reiterating his belief that words count more than ideas. Words have weight, color, sound, and endless associations.

These matters we discussed in Massachusetts Hall and returned to in Sever as we waited each Tuesday and Thursday for Professor Mercier. The questions we raised the most often could never be answered, but we enjoyed the exercise of relating them to passages in Eliot, and to our newest discovery, the poems of Mallarmé. Over lines of Mallarmé our linguistic enthusiasm reached its highest peak. I marveled at how Paul was able to clarify his thoughts in the medium of conversation. I did not possess that skill. As his voice rose in the excitement of some discovery—the opening words, for example, *ses purs ongles* of the Mallarmé sonnet—I would urge him on, without telling him that I was sinking back into the foggy space of my own thoughts.

At two o'clock in Sever, he would greet me with such a sentence as: "I am full of darkness today." It was said jauntily, but later in his rooms in the yard he would explain it by telling me he was consumed with envy of artists and thinkers, consumed with the belief that the world was a conspiracy against him. I began to hear in his words, no matter how lightly expressed, and to see in flashes that crossed his handsome face, portents I tried not to interpret.

We graduated together the next year, in June 1930. Paul returned immediately to Chicago, and I left the next day for France to spend the summer in Anjou. Urged by Paul, I felt the need to live in one of the provinces, not unrelated, as Paul pointedly said, to French literature.

He wrote to me a few times that summer. The style of those letters was "highbrow," but I refrained from telling him that in my answers. He spoke of Sever Hall and of the seeming chance that had placed us side by side in row two. The questions in his letters had always had a double meaning: lightness and realism. "Is there money in teaching?" "Is there money in writing books about Mallarmé?" "How does a man, fresh from Harvard, find highbrow students and a highbrow paying public?" I knew Paul was writing a novel, and I had learned it was better not to ask about it, and especially not to ask to see it.

Behind some of the seemingly simple sentences of those summer letters, I sensed the beginning of panic and rage: "I am reading too much ever to be a writer." "I worked late last night and my mind was filled with the myriad of minor poets and minor novelists in the world today." The Leroy family would notice a bit of depression in me whenever a letter from Chicago came. One day I tried to describe Paul to all the family. I told them that Paul was a genius with magnificent vitality who was writing a novel, and who felt defeated before the novel was finished.

Each time a letter came I was transported back to Sever Hall and especially to one of the nights when I slept on the couch in Paul's study in Massachusetts Hall. That night, exhausted by our talk, I listened to the silence of the walls around me, to the silence of the bed, the false bed where I fell asleep, and where in sleep I rediscovered my own order and knew it to be simpler and more livable than Paul's order. That night I was troubled by a vague fear for my friend. It came to me as a rhythm keeping up a perpetual beat, the strong rhythm of an opening line of a sonnet Paul and I had marveled at:

Victorieusement fui le suicide beau.

It would die down to nothing and then swell, pounding into my sleep and taking over my mind.

We had decided in our youthful pompously mannered literary conversations that no great work of literature is the work of a baffled, frustrated mind. We cited especially Dante, Shakespeare, Proust. Writers like them never attempted what they could not achieve. Their meaning was never strange to the form of their writings. Other writers, the minor ones, had minds full of unmanageable emotions. That Mallarmé sonnet, beginning with the long adverb *Victorieusement*, had literally made me—and Paul too—ill with our effort to comprehend it. But when we felt we had reached at least a partial understanding, I knew I was cured—triumphantly so—of all the experiences from which I had suffered.

The last week of that summer I was in Paris after the several weeks spent with my Angevin family, on the edge of the vineyard belonging to the Bois Planté. Paul and his mother came to Paris briefly on their way to the south of France. Mrs. Schofield was about to settle down for a period of painting under the direction of Survage, and Paul was helping her with the difficult move from Chicago to Collioures. Paul and I had one good visit: a long walk in the Luxembourg and a talk at an outside table at Le Dôme, the café closest to my Paris pension in the rue Léopold-Robert.

His natural animation was more strained, and his wit more cynical. The lighter the tone he used, the more significant were the words he spoke. Writing the novel was filling his life, and he worried that he had not scrutinized his conscience carefully enough. "Privacy is what I need," he said. "A lock on my door and a bolt on my window." And then came the dreaded question: "Am I too standard? Am I just standard fabrication?"

That question, in one of its many variants, he had asked me in row two of the Sever Hall classroom. The day in that room when Paul uttered the name of Eliot had been noumenal for me. I had slipped out of time when I heard it, and now in Paris, at the Dôme, several months later I was back in time as I heard him say: "If I were a poet, all would be easier. Prose has all the dirty words of living day by day."

We reviewed those months of our friendship—it was almost a year—and we tried to define the point we had reached in our lives in late August 1930. We found ourselves defining that point in time in terms of Sever Hall, that classroom where each of us, in turn, had sat on the chair on the platform and intoned sacred, comfortable words in French. Each of us had moved beyond the artifice of the memorized weekly speech, and we were scared as we faced the newer adventure of writing words that might one day reach a printed page and be read by an unknown public.

Of course, I did not know that day in Paris that I was never to see Paul again. Yet later when I tried to recall his very words, I could easily interpret them as a farewell speech, as sentences memorized to be given from a platform, prior to disappearing from the platform. He spoke of the need to submit to the power of the writer's imagination. Behind those words spoken by Paul at the Dôme, as behind some of the words spoken to me in the Sever classroom, I could sense a dark, dense anguish shot with light.

We said good-bye. Paul went back to Chicago where soon he married. I went to my first full-time teaching position at the Taft School in Watertown, Connecticut. His letters became fewer. After an interval of silence, his wife wrote a few lines to me to say that Paul had taken his life.

I still have the notebook in which I jotted down my first thoughts about Eliot's poems. Even in the earliest notes, and later in notations about the *Four Quartets*, I was tempted to look upon the constant elaboration he gives to the concept of time as the key to his metaphysics, as the key to his poet's message.

Time might appear in the form of a voyage, as in "The Love Song of J. Alfred Prufrock" (1915):

> Let us go then, you and I. . . .
> Shall I say, I have gone at dusk through narrow streets. . . .

Or it might appear as the moment a voyage comes to a close, as in *Ash-Wednesday* (1930):

> Here are the years that walk between. . . .
> Redeem the time. . . .

As it raises the profoundest problems of human destiny, the theme of time unites the man and the poet by joining his two missions: man as God's creature, and man as creator of song.

The name of Eliot, the theme of time, as well as the name of Mallarmé and the symbols in his poems, always bring back to mind Sever Hall and the classroom where I met Paul. His disappearance from life, and from my life, has been softened for me by the memories I have of our ardent discussions. In a way these lines that follow here are as much about him as about Eliot.

When I first read *Ash-Wednesday* in 1930, two years before Eliot came to

Harvard as lecturer and teacher, it seemed to me a religious poem, a poem of peacefulness finally reached after the earlier poems on man's human dilemmas. The announcement of a conversion in *Ash-Wednesday* seemed to coincide with a new understanding of time: "Because I know that time is always time." Those early notes and recent notes I have made about Eliot span a lifetime of reading poetry. Mallarmé and Eliot have been the surest guides for me. Twin guides, one complementing the other. I first thought of them together in the Sever classroom.

In "Burnt Norton" I learned that we can know eternity only through the concept of time (which is not eternity), and we can know salvation only through the knowledge of sin (which is the obstacle to salvation). The theme of time and the dogma of Redemption may so easily symbolize poetic effort and poetic creation that we are able to follow them as the extension or the figurative meaning of the theological matter.

Poetry is first the magnificent possibility of saying everything, as time is the perpetual possibility of salvation or damnation. Thus, poetry becomes a science — a science to be perpetually rediscovered. It is the search for a lost language. Poetry comes about when the words of poetry rediscover their lost meaning, when they undergo the chemistry of what we call "the image." Analogically Time is therefore the poetic effort, the life of poetry; and Redemption is the written poem, the work made manifest.

Of all the poets writing in English, Eliot was in his generation the closest to Mallarmé. Eliot is more explicit than Mallarmé, but he was not less tormented by the "ideal" and abstract aspect of a poem. Both knew that the poet abdicates many things when he writes. He abdicates experience in favor of form. This is an important belief of Symbolist aesthetics to which Eliot owed a great deal. Since form embraces the idea, the artist is constantly moving from the container to the contained, from the signifier to the signified, from the periphery to the center, from technique to the spirit.

In "East Coker" (1940) Eliot sees himself as the poet who has reached the middle part of his life. Each effort to use words has been a new failure. Mallarmé would not have written in such a personal way as Eliot does in this passage (fifth part of the quartet), but the point of the passage — the predestined failure of each poem — is clearly reminiscent of Mallarmé. The lonely anxiety of Baudelaire became in Mallarmé a metaphysical suffering, and so it remained in the *Quartets* of Eliot.

The poet is the fabulist who works beside time and within time. He struggles against time in order to preserve the absolute autonomy of his imagination. Even those poets of the erotic and nocturnal tradition (Mallarmé and

Eliot belong to this tradition) understand that their powers are impotent gestures because time never permits them to consider for long the pure source of poetry. Language is, at all times, a perfidious constraint. Mallarmé said this on almost every page of his work. Eliot repeated it in "East Coker" in 1940, when the world seemed about to lose everything good and great it had gained.

The metaphor of the Eliot *Quartets* is the journey in time. I believe Eliot is saying that the words of a poem may reach the Word. All poems—the *urn* of Keats, the *tombs* of Mallarmé, the *quartets* of Eliot—are experiments in thinking about poetry. The ways are many: the symbol of an object (a clown or a swan), the meaning of a dogma (eternity, the Annunciation). But the end is always the same: the conviction, the reassurance that literature is the oldest memory of man.

5. The Taft School, 1930–31

Between my senior year at Harvard, 1929–30, followed by the summer at Le Bois Planté, and my first year at graduate school, 1931–32, came the year I might easily dub my "rite of passage." A year of greater inner struggle than I have known before or since, it came later, I presume, than the usual rite of passage in a young man's life. I was twenty-one, almost twenty-two, sentimentally excited over my last days in Paris and my literary survey of its streets and cafés and churches, and the proud possessor of my first contract as teacher, a year's contract to teach at the Taft School, in Watertown, Connecticut, one of the five or six best preparatory schools in the Northeast. The offer had come before I had left for my summer in France, and I had accepted it on the strong advice of my two mentors at Harvard: Professors Morize and Mercier. Throughout the summer weeks spent in Paris and Anjou and Paris again, I had given it very little thought. But a sense of security—at least for a year—had allowed me to enjoy France better than I might have, if no job had awaited me in September. More than security, the excitement of turning full-time teacher, and teaching a subject I had been training myself to teach, made the boat trip home seem tedious and long.

I drove from Brookline to Watertown in my second car—a Chevy—and on arrival paid my respects immediately to Horace Dutton Taft, founder and headmaster of the school—a very tall, soft-spoken, dignified man, obviously proud of his school and skillful in making newcomers feel at home. But I sensed that after the warm welcome, business would start up immediately.

Masters and pupils would be expected to behave in ways fitting their station. When Mr. Taft said to me, as he stood in the doorway of his immense living room, "You are our only new master this year, and you will be observed overtly and covertly in many ways and for some time. Be yourself. You will like it here," he might have been speaking to a freshman. At least he made me feel like one.

In just a few days the pattern of my new life was fixed: classes and other duties, my small apartment adequately furnished at the end of a long corridor of which I was supervisor or "master in charge," the large study hall where I was supposed to keep order from seven to nine o'clock one evening a week, my table in the dining room for nine pupils and myself and where each week one set of pupils would leave my table and nine others would join me. Thus gradually I would get to know most of the students.

I was decidedly the youngest master, and at the beginning made to feel that by the other masters and the pupils, and, whenever I encountered him, by Mr. Taft. There were advantages and disadvantages in that situation which I soon recorded in my mind, and then tried to reflect in my behavior.

Taft School prepared the majority of its students, at least its brightest students, for Yale. There were strong bonds between the school and the university, and endless talk, even in September, of the probability or improbability of getting into Yale. The fundamental reasons were not academic or athletic, but social. Yale would be, if reached, the continuing of a tradition in which a Taft graduate would feel at home. Here I was, fresh from Harvard, unaccountably admitted to a foreign stronghold. The gibes and jokes about my presence, my invasion, gradually wore thin as masters and pupils grew accustomed to seeing me there among them, seemingly permanent in my new office of master.

I was given four classes to teach: three sections of beginning French, four days a week, and one section of second-year French, four days a week. Sixteen hours in the classroom, with fifteen students in each class. Thus I had all the freshmen who had elected beginning French, and fifteen sophomores who were trying a second year at the language. In a way I was a freshman too, and that helped to make our almost daily meetings harmonious. We were all starting off together, exploring a new land, in a state that was new for many of us, although our tight schedules allowed us only a little freedom on weekends to walk about Watertown and possibly the neighboring town of Waterbury.

There were no freshmen on my corridor. The juniors and seniors who occupied the twenty or so rooms that fell under my jurisdiction formed a territory for which I was clearly responsible. But all of the forty students living there, during those hours when they were freest to sleep or study or engage in pranks or general roughhousing, were not necessarily responsible citizens. Politely, and at times not so politely, they set about testing me, to see how far they might go in their life on my corridor: how much noise they could make in the showers, what language they might get away with as they walked or ran down the corridor, and what degree of nudity they might demonstrate in the corridor as they moved between the showers and their rooms.

Several of them—the strongest and the most athletic-looking—were out-and-out exhibitionists and fully aware of the pleasure they had in exhibiting themselves to their frailer classmates, and to me. The word "macho" had not come into use at that time, but it would have applied to the naked strutting in the corridor. If I happened to pass, their overpolite "Good morning, sir" was in contrast with the pride in their maleness which they hoped would cover up their breaking a rule.

I decided that too much attention paid to their infringements might lead to more and more infringements and to a gloating over my reprimands. I tried, therefore, to establish some kind of friendly relations with my neighbors. Some of them were taking the upper-class French courses, and they began to consult me in my study. Then others used their English compositions or even history papers as devices to "drop in" between seven and ten. Finally, brief visits would occur without need for consultations. Here the fact that I had studied at Harvard counted heavily. Many of the Taft students were anxious (secretly) to ask about the rival university in Cambridge, or about university life in general. The two summers I had spent in France were also topics that provided for questions and answers and speculations.

I attended the daily chapel service that immediately preceded dinner. It was brief: the singing of a hymn, a prayer, and announcements for the entire student body, followed by a five- to seven-minute talk, almost always given by the headmaster. Mr. Taft was alone on the platform. This was his part of the day. Histrionically he pulled the community together by his towering stature, by the paternal gentle-firmness of his manner, and by the elegance of his speech. We were reminded daily that this was his school, that he had shaped it into an institution of which he was proud, and that all of us, if we were to stay within its walls, would have to adjust to and even exult in the rules of study, behavior, morality, and speech that he had set up and exemplified. During those ten or fifteen minutes he was both chief of the tribe and medicine man. We quieted down then during those minutes, and I imagined that every one of us in the chapel felt grateful for being in that place at that moment of our lives. Dignified to the right degree, yes, he was that, but he also enjoyed reciting his jokes. He demonstrated warmth of feeling when we were all together, and there was no danger of sentimentality. But with us individually he was detached and strongly apprehensive of allowing any sentimentality in his own nature to be expressed.

On Sundays I attended mass in the parish church of Watertown. There were several pupils from the school and Mr. Reardon, the history teacher who was, I imagine, the most admired master at Taft. I sat alone in my favorite spot in front on what we used to call the "Gospel" side of the nave. Families from the town were all around me, adults and children who had nothing to do with Taft School, who could not suspect the minor dramas I was becoming engaged in during the other days of the week. I was a stranger to them. We were there for the same reason—to worship—and to forget the daily occupations of work and family. Mass was an opening out on to something bigger than Taft, than Watertown, than the congregation of pupils and families in the church. It was an escape into a world that surrounds the world and gives it meaning. Each Sunday it helped to stabilize me into a sense of proportions and values. If a few of the pupils joined me as we walked back to the school, we might speak of such matters, and then later in the week the subject of religion would be joined with other subjects in the evening visits in my study.

Many of those evenings were solitary vigils when I prepared work for the next day and assessed the happenings of the day just ended. Why was I there in that place? Would I stay there? Where would I go if I left? Would the excitement I felt each morning in teaching French to those youngsters last through the years ahead? Was my temperament suited to such an enclosed life, so closely patterned on a monastic life? Time for reading had been drastically cut, and it was being taken up by the lives of those students in my classes who needed extra drilling, and by the other students on my corridor who consulted me as an older friend. I was losing sight of myself and losing contact with my own mind. A master at Taft was not solely that: he was a body to be used at any hour of the day or night for routines, exercises, and for emergencies.

The day began at seven A.M. when I heard the first showers turned on, far down the corridor, and the first doors opened or slammed shut. From then on, anything might happen: a fight in the shower room, with screams of "rape, rape," or a boy's room being messed up by other boys in search of some ill-defined vengeance. At breakfast there might be slight skirmishes, and, if I intervened, grumblings against me as a kind of scapegoat. The classroom was a quieter place. There I did not have to seek control. It came naturally through the work. Those boys wanted to learn French. They wanted good grades. They wanted to get into Yale. They wanted to visit Paris and see for themselves if the Louvre, if Notre Dame, if la Place Pigalle were all they were supposed to be.

Afternoons were for exercise and sports, for laboratory work and study. The chapel service had a quieting effect that usually lasted through dinner when the conversation might be of a somewhat higher order. Study hour until nine or ten was an oasis of peacefulness at the end of which I had to be on the alert for the unexpected. Roughhousing was the blatant form which, if it weren't put down immediately, could grow to out-and-out rebellion.

The covert form of misdemeanor was sexual, either forced and semi-sadistic, or secretive: a rendezvous behind closed doors for mutual pleasure. Since I had to check presences in rooms at various times, doors were not locked, and I did come upon a few such engagements. Neither Mr. Taft nor any of the older masters had given me instructions concerning my duty about such matters. But I knew from talk I had overheard that if I reported the boys, they would be expelled. I never did make such a report, but chose to discuss the "situation" with the two boys when the first moment of their fear had quieted down, and when my own embarrassment had diminished. I can no longer remember what I said. It was just "talk," I think. If it happened to be, as it was in a few instances, an obvious seduction of a freshman by a senior, I became a stern advisor. Although I remember one freshman saying to me: "You've got it all wrong, sir, I was putting the make on Jimmie!"

When invited to Mr. Taft's house, which was a wing of the principal building, it was usually with a few students and perhaps another master or two. This might be for sherry before Sunday dinner, or dinner on a Saturday night. He was a gracious host, smiling during questions about the school and about his famous family. He always recalled anecdotes connected with the school, but we knew that by coffee time he was inexorably moving toward his recitation of the Gilbert and Sullivan operas. The entire repertory was in his head. Their jingling humor never failed to amuse him. Impressed by his memory at first, I soon grew tired of the recitations which always went on too long. Of course they did fill out the hour allotted for our presence in Mr. Taft's living room. I often wished he would turn to Pope and Shelley, to Poe or Whitman. But Mr. Taft was not basically a literary man. He loved American history and knew it well. Those Gilbert texts from *H.M.S. Pinafore* and *The Mikado*, and from the most obscure, rarely performed works, were a firm tradition at Taft, and the boys, even if they grew tired, as I did, of the lengthy recitations, continued to admire their headmaster's memory.

To clear my head of those rhymes and rhythms, once back in my study I would take down from my bookshelf the copy of Eliot's poems I had bought in Cambridge the year before, and would read out loud "Cousin Harriet" and "Prufrock," and those parts of "The Waste Land" I had been studying and felt I was beginning to understand. I would think then of my classmate Paul Schofield who in Professor Mercier's French course had told me first about the importance of T. S. Eliot. Memories of Harvard, then, would crowd about me: Professor Babbitt on Rousseau, Professor Kittredge on Shakespeare, Professor Kirsup Lake reading the eschatological chapter 24 from Matthew, Paul's room in Massachusetts Hall where we would try to decipher Mallarmé's sonnets.

Taft School and Harvard: two worlds related and yet so different. Not unlike the two parts of my nature, the two warring parts that never gave me rest: my austere self and the lascivious one; my sense of duty and my yearning for adventure; miserliness and generosity; my reticent self and my confiding self; my love of the Bible and my strong attraction to Nietzsche. After two months at Taft, I began fearing the enjoyment I felt in teaching first- and second-year French. That kind of teaching came from coddling, nurturing those boys as they began to articulate and speak French, as they began to read and write in a language that moved them away from the familiar setting of Watertown and from the history of New England.

Reading those Eliot poems in my bed at night before turning out the light was a return to Harvard where Eliot had once studied. It gave me an appetite for another kind of teaching—in a university world where the study of a poem in a foreign language would justify the study of the language. A poem can change a man's life. I had been born out of my mother, but I reasoned with myself that I was perhaps being guided by generations and centuries before her. The flotsam of language, the triviality of language was all about me each day, but I was already losing my heart and my mind to those epic trunks of language I had found in the books of Proust and Joyce.

I dwell in Possibility. That line of Emily Dickinson kept returning to me when during my free moments each day I tried to pierce the future to see what I wanted and what I was capable of. How solitary I was that year surrounded and hemmed in by so many swift-moving lithe bodies and by so many older bodies who gave me advice concerning the disasters that were to befall me my first year at Taft, most of which did not occur! My secret mental life, when I was able to give it free rein, took me back to Europe, and I would travel fawningly in the wake of Pound and Eliot. The American in Paris. A younger Prufrock, not surrounded by ladies speaking of a great artist, but moving from café to café in search of those who had sought and found before him.

More and more numerous they grew, my reveries of escape, not from women at tea parties, but from those youths who ravenously fixed on a young teacher who knew nothing of their childhood but knew everything about their present dreams and drives.

A double life held me then: the life of a teacher—a public man observed from breakfast on through the day until the last round was made at ten o'clock and the jailer could retreat to his own bed—and the inner life of a reader who was tracking down ghosts of himself as he recited "Prufrock" and the Mallarmé sonnets, and as he studied the patterns of myth and music in "The Waste Land" and *Ulysses*. I moved ceaselessly between yearning and intellectual detachment. Whenever a powerful emotion took hold of me, I set about searching for and finding an equally powerful check on that emotion. In this, Eliot's case was before me at all times. I wanted to encounter all my personal demons, and I felt simultaneously the need to control them. I did not brood over the pattern of my life, but I tried to see it, and to understand what Babbitt in his classroom the year before had called the evils of romanticism.

In a solitary way I lived between two kinds of texts, between two languages: the poems of Eliot and those of Mallarmé. From them I learned what was to become for me the central lesson about the art of a poem. Reticence is the source of great lyric power. They were difficult poems for me during that year at Taft, and today, a half-century later, they are still difficult poems, but in their familiarity they have grown into a part of my psyche. They helped my psyche in its groping toward some illuminations concerning the mysteries of God's world. My memory of the past has been so continuously, day after day, woven around those texts, that often the past seems to me one day. One single day I am still living and still questioning.

In both Eliot and Mallarmé I believed I found a tragic intuition of aloneness. But if that were the subject of "Prufrock" and "L'Après-midi d'un faune," the solitary man had become a poet in the discipline of his art and in the dedication of his art. In order to offset the bustling life in and out of classrooms, in and out of study halls and dining rooms, on and off athletic fields in the afternoons, I took refuge in certain texts that allowed me to meditate on what made a great writer. Eliot had taught briefly in England, and Mallarmé had taught English in lycées most of his life. The more I learned of the biographies of these men, the more I realized how the writer—at least a writer of their stature—is a many-minded identity. In each of the poems I tried to explore, even in the obvious mythical poems such as "The Waste Land" and "Hérodiade," I knew that the poet was insisting on the reality of his experience. How such intimations helped me!

A few years later, after my experience at Taft School, without ever leaving

Eliot and Mallarmé behind, I moved into the work of two other poets—Dante and Baudelaire—and soon realized that all four poets were closely, intimately related. the *Inferno* and *Les Fleurs du Mal* created a much bolder atmosphere of that terror and mystery in which our life is passed. But "The Hollow Men" and "Le pitre châtié" had given me a premonition of that atmosphere. In my classroom at Taft and in the endless conversations I had with those very young students, I relied on that regulated life which was carried out, on the whole, in an atmosphere of great friendliness. There, in many guises, everything we said or did was in terms of hope in the future, in preparation for a future career. Poetry is not about the future. It is about what has been lived consciously and unconsciously in the past.

Thus I learned at Taft a lesson, even a doctrine, that has never ceased being real to me. Present time is nonexistent. What we call the present is in reality the past which is being remembered, or the future which is being fantasized. The present is composed of impulses to turn back and remember, and other impulses to look ahead into pictures of achievement where all of a man's efforts will be rewarded and recognized. Euphoria! I was not at all unlike those boys who were franker with me when they spoke of their dreams than I was with them when I tried to pull them into a fictional present of conjugations and vocabulary. In their own adolescent wisdom they knew that the tiresome drills were to lead to a discovery of their own personality as they read of the personality of Corneille or Flaubert concealed in the printed pages of *Le Cid* or *Un coeur simple.*

My Taft students did not brood over the pattern of their lives, but I brooded over mine. They knew that this was the best of all presents for them, and they accepted the pattern with some degree of pride and even gratitude. Revolt and revulsion against the school, if they occurred, were momentary. A conversation with one of the masters, even with me, would ease their hurt spirit, and the future would appear so glowing that they accepted the tedium of day-to-day life. Most of my conversations were for that purpose: to correct some kind of grumbling and to bolster a flagging spirit. But I had no one to turn to for an exchange of words that might lessen my own fits of brooding. And that is why the poems of Eliot loomed large for me. I too knew something of the "modern attitudes" Eliot describes in "Cousin Nancy." I too had something of that Puritan inheritance of skepticism and conscientiousness. I too had more than a little of Prufrock's hesitating nature and indecisiveness.

The test came in the early spring in the form of a letter from Professor J. D. M. Ford, chairman of Romance languages, a somewhat awesome figure at Harvard whom I had often seen entering or leaving Widener Library. It was the offer of an instructorship and the chance to begin graduate work. My mind and my deepest instinct said yes to this letter I had been expecting. But another part of me, my heart, I suppose, that nature in me disliking risks, had already adjusted to the regimentation of Taft School, to conversations with boys that started with French and France, and led to deeper problems of life and love and vocation. I had grown accustomed to the wholeness of existence in that Connecticut school, where every hour was accounted for. There were minor infractions against the semi-monastic and sturdily moralistic pattern of that life. But they were quickly corrected or forgotten in the general flood of affirmations and the need to study for each class each day.

Two, three days passed before I went to Mr. Taft—the first time I made a formal appointment. By then I had made up my mind to return to Harvard. The headmaster urged me to stay one more year, to make sure that Taft was not the style of life I would want ultimately. He thought it might well be. And of course he was right. It was our most painful conversation. Mr. Taft knew that part of me wanted to stay on, and that part of me felt the duty to train myself in the mysterious ways of a doctorate. I would be following my duty too if I stayed at Taft where the art of teaching would involve far greater skills and tests than college teaching. There too he was right and I floundered about in my ill-formed, ill-articulated arguments.

His very large body, as it sank into a thronelike armchair, the serenity of his face, crossed on this occasion by fleeting expressions of sternness, the arguments he used which seemed watertight to him and too reasonable for this flighty young Harvard man refusing his offer of a one-way trip to Paradise — all of this made me out to be ungrateful, stubborn, uncompromising, and stupid. A moment came, in those hour-long minutes, when Mr. Taft must have realized he was wasting his time. He closed the session with a kingly gesture of his hand: "Write to me in a day or two your decision. Remember that I want you to stay and the boys want you to stay. This school could be your home."

Late that night, when my charges were sleeping and the corridor was peaceful, I went outside and walked to the back of the main building and to the playing field that lay beyond it. The moon was a great source of light behind the trees that lined the field. It was a concourse of stars that night, and I was alone watching it, feeling my aloneness in the decision I had to make, and feeling at the same time the total insignificance of that drama weighing down on me . . . *Le silence éternel de ces espaces infinis.* How good it was to experience the terror of that space and to dissipate the paltriness of my worry! The infinity of night helped my reason waging its struggle over my heart.

I looked back at the buildings of Taft School outlined against the sky. At that moment, and for the first time, I think, they spelled out the word "captivity." That was the image they called up. It was not threatening or harsh. I knew that captivity had been benevolent for me, as it was for some of the students. For John Morrissey, for example, who in my second-year French course, had serenely accepted the prisonlike pattern of daily life, had triumphed over it by adjusting to it, and had known, perhaps subconsciously, that such a school is indeed a miniature of human existence in a community with its fluctuations of fortune: defeats and triumphs. On Sundays I often sat beside John at mass, when I imagine for both of us the school fell into a saner perspective.

A sense of captivity often grew in the minds of freshmen and sophomores with the result of slight revolts or at least critical blusterings. Then in the third and fourth years the opposite thought began to take over: perhaps it is a good place and the next place may be more painful. They began then to feel more at home in the penitentiary and even preferred it in ways to the real home with which they kept in touch by telephone. They were beginning to enjoy by then the comradeship of a few good friends sharing the cells and classrooms, the food and the exercise, the study hall and the bull sessions. Such experiences were already turning into memories which were telling them: it is not a bad life even if it is not unlike a jail.

That evening I was the new master, on the point of leaving, as if his sentence had come to an end. He was sad with the thought that the fresh memories he held of that year would soon lose their freshness and gradually sink into oblivion. Would he want to return to the penitentiary? Would he regret leaving the familiar world of masters, of menus, of freshman hesitations, and of serious self-assurances?

6. Saint Benoît-du-Lac

A year after my semester at Albertus Magnus, in the spring of 1944 (I was still teaching at Yale but coming to the end of a five-year contract), I made plans to spend Holy Week in Canada, at a Benedictine monastery, Saint Benoît-du-Lac, just outside of Montreal. This desire was somewhat related to my experience at Albertus Magnus, but it had grown in me largely because of constant urging by a student at Yale, Keith Botsford, not literally a student in one of my classes but one who called on me often in my Trumbull College apartment and who brought with him an abundant enthusiasm for literature. He was only a freshman but extraordinarily well-read and had a very special devotion to the Catholic Church. He had taken me on—I forget how we met—as a new friend worthy of sharing his passion for literature and for the Church. In fact I was the only one of his circle with whom he could talk seriously about his faith, and especially about this Benedictine monastery where he had made many retreats.

In two ways I succumbed to Keith's insistence and persistence. Often when he called, I would say, "I must work, can't see you today." He would pay no attention to those words and launch into some outrageous theory about the style of James Joyce. If I denounced his theory, I was caught in his trap. An hour later he would take up again the theme of Saint Benoît-du-Lac and try to convince me how important it was for my entire future for me to go there and live for a few days in that atmosphere.

Keith had two very contradictory plans for my future. One was for me to marry his mother, an Italian lady whose husband had died, and the other was to see me clothed in the black habit of a Benedictine monk. I never knew how he reconciled those two projects, but logic was never a stumbling block for Keith. I introduced him to two students who were studying French literature with me: Roger Shattuck and Harvey Shapiro, both equally keen on literary study and on developing their own writing powers. They formed a triumvirate, with 1248 Trumbull as a center. I had the deep satisfaction of watching all three turn into writers, teachers, and editors, and seeing them sustain through the years a warm friendship for one another.

Several weeks before Holy Week in 1944, I secured permission by letter from the monastery in Canada to spend the seven days as a guest of the order. The "lake" in the title is Magog, and a bus from Montreal took me there. It was a bright sunny day and the large semi-Gothic building was awesome. A monk met me at the entrance and showed me my room (a small cell-like room) on the third floor. He gave me a program of the hours, when they would be sung in the chapel, showed me the large refectory, and told me to come early for supper that first evening. If I wished to be assigned a spiritual director, he would arrange for that. The introduction to what my life was to be for the week, through Easter Sunday, was so efficiently carried out that I realized these Benedictines received a large number of visitors. And I imagined they were more concerned with the young men who arrived as possible postulants and novices than with visitors like myself bent on hearing plainsong and watching the liturgical services.

As I wandered about that first day—there was about an hour before suppertime—I felt years away from 1944, back in a medieval world of austerity. Before I was assigned a seat at the visitors' table in the refectory, I was conducted to the center of the large room, washed my hands in a basin held by a monk, and then the Father Superior dried my hands and welcomed me. The bowl of soup followed by a plate of deliciously cooked vegetables made me feel guilty as I could easily see the monks eating very little. I quickly perceived the difference between the older men dressed in black habits who were monks and priests, and some of the younger men in brown habit, who were novices or brothers. There was no conversation during the meal, but we listened to the reading in French of some appropriate texts.

That evening I attended Compline and heard for the first time at Saint Benoît-du-Lac the expert singing of plainchant by those monks who, I was not surprised to learn, had been trained by the monks at Solesmes. With the singing of the hymns and psalms, the lights were gradually extinguished, and then, one by one, as each finished his private prayers, the monks and brothers left the choir. I was the last to leave the chapel that evening.

The next morning I did not attend the first hour of Matins and Prime, at four o'clock, but I made it to mass at six. After breakfast I explored the property, watched the gardening going on, and visited the cheese factories. Wherever I stopped someone would talk with me and provide the few explanations I needed. The other canonical hours were usually grouped in twos and sung together: Tierce and Sext, the Angelus and Vespers. I looked forward to those services of sound and prayer, as the days went by, and estimated that about four hours each day were spent in the chapel at prayer and contemplation of God. The Gregorian chant was done impeccably. It was medieval and sung by those twentieth-century men who at regular intervals interrupted their work in the fields or in the factory or in the kitchen to come together to sing and pray.

The hours and the days passed quickly. As soon as one liturgical event was over or one period of work came to an end, another was being prepared. A fairly wild lonely countryside separated the monastery buildings from local communities. I imagined several acres represented the official enclosure. As I wandered about in total freedom, my mind rehearsed steadily all I was observing and experiencing: the deprivation in these men of normal appetites —food, sleep, sex, and communication with others. Because of that regimen, and despite their empty Lenten stomachs, despite the long slow hours in choir, this liturgical life was what they wanted, what they had chosen. Such a medieval ordering of life provided the productive darkness of contemplation.

As far as I could see, the monks at Saint Benoît had avoided the always possible danger of indulging in the romanticism of religious life, the romanticism even of its rigor and monotonies. They enjoyed their life without constantly asking the question, "Should it be enjoyed?" I was the romantic there when I said to myself from time to time, "I wish they wore white like the Trappists." I was the romantic when at dinner I contrasted the status of the visitors like myself as we ate from a plate of well-cooked vegetables, accompanied by fresh bread and cheese, with that of the monks at their table who dunked a chunk of dried bread into a bowl of soup. They were contemplatives and at the same time they were energetic men, endowing their community with strong vitality. My thoughts often turned to Carthusians and the bit I knew of La Grande Chartreuse. And then I thought wryly of my semi-monastic life at Trumbull College and Sterling Library. In comparison with my life, these men had learned to turn away from self-will and seek God's will.

There were good moments of quasi-contemplation on my part, and other moments filled with questions my mind kept turning over. What had brought me here? Was it the exhortations of Keith? Or was it something beyond him? Can a writer exist as such and be estranged from the world? Are these men really estranged? Or are they in their meditations closer to the center of humanity than the rest of us who live in the midst of seeming activity and seeming usefulness? Christian thought had always taught me to believe that no unexpected encounter is accidental. This contemplative experience I was having could not be explained by chance or whim.

The three services of Tenebrae that ended the day's program on Wednesday, Thursday, and Friday, and replaced the singing of Compline, moved me more than any others that week. What a prodigious place the Psalms have in Christian worship! In the literal meaning of the Psalms we seem to be connected with Exodus. At the end of the singing of a psalm, a candle was put out, and we were being led from the literalness of the words to some spiritual understanding. Easter and the Passover were coming closer each night, and I thought of the blood of the paschal lamb placed on the lintel of the door. At the end of each of the three evenings the last candle, the only one left lighted, was carried behind the altar and there extinguished with the sound of a crash. Then, one by one, the monks rose from their knees and left the chapel.

During the daytime I would see on the faces of those monks and brothers expressions of boyishness and lightheartedness. In the orchards, the barns, and the factories, there was a sense of contentment in the community. But questions kept returning to my mind during the hours of devotion in the chapel when the faces of the monks were not clearly visible, and when I wondered about the few with whom I had spoken and a few others I had observed. Despite their air of happiness, did they suffer at times from acedia, from spiritual sloth, the traditional problem of monks (according to Baudelaire)? Did they think of going into other orders, becoming Carthusians, Cistercians, Franciscans, Jesuits? Like Jonah, did they feel trapped inside a whale? I had studied Evelyn Underhill's books on mysticism the two ways in Christian thought: affirmation and rejection. Was the monastic life too rigorously the way of rejection? Both ways are possible. In the world, passion and reason occupy us too much.

Pascal's lesson on "diversions" (*les divertissements*), when I first read those *pensées*, had spoken to me directly and coincided with what I sensed before reading them and had not fully articulated to myself. At the end of each of the Tenebrae offices, I felt almost within that elected world of silence and obedience. I felt that my time-bound self was almost lost in union with God. I have to say "almost" because I was still the observer, the guest, the outsider.

The monks ahead of me in their choir were living the vow of stability. By contrast, I was still within a meaningless mobility.

I learned especially that week in Canada that a monastery is not a home. It is not rooted as a home is. It is a place where a man disappears from the world in order to be everywhere in the world, thanks to his passion and to his state of being hidden. Some years later, in reading Thomas Merton and Flannery O'Connor, I was to pay attention to the aloneness of those writers, one in a monastery and the other outside. With their examples I learned how their faith grew in that aloneness where they refined their talent and deepened their love of God.

Saturday morning came at Saint Benoît-du-Lac, and with it an almost joyous high mass at eleven, in reality, I suppose, the first mass of Easter. After the consecration, a small procession passed by me down the central aisle of the church. (That morning there were so many visitors attending mass that the church was used rather than the chapel.) I was amazed to see, carried on a raft by four monks, a lamb, securely tied and bleating. When the procession reached the main altar, there was a brief interruption in the singing, and the celebrant turned to the lamb and blessed it. Then the victim was carried down the other aisle out of the church. This was, I learned later, an early medieval monastic ceremony carried out on Holy Saturday. Sunday lunch, following Easter high mass, was roast lamb.

Those two days, Saturday and Sunday, were crowded with solemn services, and jubilant with great freedom in conversation. Late Sunday afternoon I took the bus back to Montreal, but before that, I met and talked with members of the families of the religious, for whom there was a reception after lunch. A few of the brothers spoke to me for the first time and introduced me to some members of their family. They asked me how I liked the monastery, what I thought of it after living there one week. One of them said to me: "Of course from time to time we are oppressed by the silence and the loneliness and the absence of women. But that oppression we have felt also in the world, and here it never lasts long. Here we become more ourselves."

As we talked that afternoon in a jovial, almost mirthful way, my mind stole back quietly to the best moments I had had during the week: to the night offices especially and the Gregorian chant, to the closest I had come to understanding the contemplative cast of mind, to my meditations on the ways of affirmation and rejection in the Christian life, to the great energy and attention that is needed in the experience of solitude.

7. Albertus Magnus

I had walked many times by the large white house on St. Ronan's Street before learning that it was Albertus Magnus College for young women, run by the Sisters of St. Dominic. The house had always seemed to me a bit more graceful in its architecture than most of the New Haven houses of that size. And the street itself—with its name that always reminded me of Ernest Renan, because Ronan is an older Breton form of Renan—seemed more peaceful, more sedate than other streets that surrounded Yale, where at the time of this story I was into my third year of teaching.

During my first two years I had come to St. Ronan Street to attend gatherings of students and colleagues at the apartment of Henri and Marguerite Peyre. I knew then only the first part of the street, before one would come upon Albertus Magnus, and only at night. My daytime walks this third year usually had a goal, if I continued on past the college and came to East Rock Road which crossed St. Ronan. There, almost at the intersection, was the house of a new friend, Catherine Coffin, who had recently moved to New Haven where her younger son Bill was soon to attend Yale. We had met almost fortuitously at the Alliance Française. It was Catherine in fact who had explained to me to what use the big white house on St. Ronan Street, close to her street, had been put.

One day in the fall semester I was talking with my friend and colleague Andy Morehouse in his office at Pierson College. We were pleasantly interrupted by the arrival of a beautiful nun, Sister Marie-Louise, dressed in her

Dominican habit of white and black. She came with a difficult bibliographical question about Pascal, the subject of the doctoral dissertation she was doing under Andy's direction. Thus I had the privilege of meeting a member of the community of Albertus Magnus. We exchanged words about Pascal, the teaching of college French, and the large white house on St. Ronan Street.

That evening Sister Marie-Louise telephoned me to ask if I would stop by Albertus Magnus the next day or two and speak with the Sister-President. The reason for that conversation was an invitation to give a course in the spring on "modern literature," readings of my own choice, which might interest a small group of senior girls. Thus I became familiar with the white house, a refuge for me from the many duties and activities that engaged me at Yale. It was my introduction to a Catholic college and to an atmosphere of peace where everyone was respectful of everyone else. I met few sisters save Sister Marie-Louise, who served as friend and guide and French colleague, and very few students save those eight or ten who sat with me in a small classroom where we discussed some texts of Baudelaire and Eliot, of Sartre and Graham Greene, of Nietzsche and Rimbaud. The students, quite accustomed to have Yale teachers give them a course now and then, were a delight to teach. They were relaxed and intelligent. By the end of the semester we were good friends.

The house on St. Ronan Street was a dedicated place. Each time I entered it, twice a week that spring semester, I sensed that dedication. It inspired me and changed me. I was being healed in some mysterious way. The smiles on the faces of the students and on the faces of the sisters were different from the smiles I saw elsewhere in New Haven.

My oldest friend in that city, or just outside that city in Mount Carmel, Mabel Lafarge, was pleased that I was having the experience of teaching at Albertus Magnus. I had known her since coming to Yale two and a half years earlier, and called on her regularly either alone or with a group of students. When alone we often spoke of her conversion to the Church, of the great change that had made in her life. She had always been attentive to my work at Yale, and hospitable to my students who asked her questions about her uncle, Henry Adams, and her brother-in-law, the Jesuit priest John Lafarge. But she seemed more interested than ever in knowing about the course I gave at Albertus Magnus, about the attitude of students there, and about the Dominican sisters.

Catherine Coffin, my new friend, was equally interested, although more in terms of pedagogy. I was able, through those months I taught at Albertus Magnus, to rehearse with my two friends, who had never met, my impressions of the new experience. Older than me and wiser, they were, especially during that season of my third year, ministering hands, patient, thoughtful, encouraging. Each in her own way was caught up with French culture. And each, in her own way, released my rehearsal of experiences in France, the account of my courses at Yale, and the account of my newest experience in the white house on St. Ronan Street. A class of girls, and Catholic girls at that, offset my classes of boys at Yale, and related me to my recent past at Bennington where most of my students had been girls. But they were two very different worlds, Bennington and Albertus Magnus, and I enjoyed discussing those differences with Mabel and Catherine.

The semester was approaching its end. For commencement that year, the sisters had invited an eminent Catholic woman to speak—Clare Boothe Luce —and the community was proud that Mrs. Luce had accepted. My two friends from Mount Carmel and East Rock Road had accepted my invitation to attend the ceremony, and I was eager to have them finally meet.

Four days before the commencement—it was to be held in the evening in one of the Yale buildings—the Sister-President telephoned me to say that a sudden illness would prevent Mrs. Luce from coming to New Haven. "Will you," she asked, "speak in her place, on this very short notice? You have taught a few of the graduating seniors and the others know of you. You could help us out in this emergency." Unaccustomed to giving that kind of talk, I accepted, but with serious misgivings. After I told Mabel Lafarge and Catherine Coffin of the unexpected role I would have at the exercise, they assured me they would still come and do without my service of escort. Then I went into a two-day retreat to plan what I would say to the students, in the presence of parents and faculty.

On the evening of the ceremony, all those who were to march in the procession congregated in the lobby outside the hall. The seniors, the administrators, and I were standing about waiting for the signal to form ranks and enter the hall. A young lady approached to say there was an urgent telephone call for me. The telephone was fortunately in the lobby. I answered, and heard Mabel Lafarge's voice, faint but audible.

"I am sorry," she was saying, "but I will not be able to come to the commencement this evening. I fell ill this morning."

I was urging her to stay quiet and recover as fast as she could, but she went on speaking: "No, it is not an ordinary illness. You see, I am going to die tonight and I wanted to tell you it is all right. It is as I wanted it to be, and I am prepared. Goodbye, God bless."

Stunned, I took my place in the procession, which began moving. Half doubting, half believing Mabel's words spoken on the telephone, I listened to the exercises, spoke my piece, noticed in the audience Catherine sitting with a friend, and at the end moved with the procession out of the hall and walked back to my rooms at Trumbull College.

There was no notice of Mrs. Lafarge's death in the morning paper. But she had died about three in the morning. This I learned from Father Lawrason Riggs, Yale chaplain for Catholic students, or rather from Father Riggs's man-servant, Silk, to whom I telephoned at nine that morning.

Serenely she died, my oldest friend during my first years at Yale, and with full knowledge she was dying. The funeral mass was celebrated in New Haven by her brother-in-law, Father John Lafarge, whom I had met several times at Mabel's house. I remember the slowness of his steps at the altar, the dignity his words and movements gave the mass. Her friends, almost none of whom was Catholic, were present that morning at St. Mary's.

I had a few minutes alone with Father Lafarge and told him of her last words to me on the telephone. He did not seem surprised by that message and its accurate prediction. He brushed that aside and spoke rather of Albertus Magnus and of Mabel's approval of my teaching there. She reasoned, he told me, that each must be doing the other good: the teacher and the college. Yale was secularized; Albertus Magnus was still attached to the spirit of St. Dominic.

The white-house-turned-college on St. Ronan Street was my first entrance into a purely Catholic world. At the beginning of that spring semester, I was the observer of the wide hallway with the staircase at the back, of the few offices where I spoke briefly with the president and the dean, and my classroom—small but adequate for the ten girls, who arrived promptly for our afternoon class and chatted with me easily and eagerly about their college and their courses, New Haven and Connecticut, and their plans for the coming year. Gradually, as the semester went on, I felt myself becoming a participant in that atmosphere so clearly set off from the rest of the city. I had a function to perform there twice a week. I was expected, and as the weeks went on I grew more and more eager to meet that expectation as best I could.

I spoke of Albertus Magnus only with my two friends: Mabel, whose death was to be so strangely connected with it; and Catherine, always interested in it but hesitant to accept what I said about the effect of the religious atmosphere on me. Even Mabel, who had been brought up in the Unitarian Church, was in her own way hesitant too. Although Mabel had been in the Catholic Church longer than I had been, she knew, as I knew, that converts never fully recover from an early training in their lives that tells them there is something sinister about Catholicism, something wrong about the display of crucifixes and holy statues. A questioning hesitancy always lingers in the convert which a born Catholic never feels—even the Catholic who has lost his faith. I find traces of this hesitancy in the writings even of such famous converts as Jacques Maritain and Thomas Merton, whose lives were so totally transformed by the Church.

I knew that the quiet I felt in the atmosphere of Albertus Magnus was not forced, nor was the cheerfulness in the attitudes and behavior of the sisters. I knew finally beyond any doubt that I was entering into the movement of that gravitation which is the life and the spirit of God, that center who is everywhere. Something opened up inside me. I needed silence, and yet I was supposed to speak on entering the college building. I caught myself saying inwardly: this will lead me to the male world of a monastery.

I sought the power of volition to liberate myself from everything visible. My teaching was the same, but the spirit behind it had changed. Albertus Magnus was the closest I had come to the atmosphere of a retreat, of a monastery, of solitude and silence where the noise of the world does not reach. This was 1943. Forty years later, in 1983, I read that it was in 1941 that Thomas Merton made the long train ride from New York to Kentucky, to the Trappists, the Cistercians of the Strict Observance, and the Abbey of Our Lady of Gethsemane. There he observed the monks kneeling in their choir, in their white cowls, praying for the agonized world and bringing Christ closer to the world.

8. Yaddo

I heard the strange name first in Vermont in the late thirties when I was teaching at Bennington College. A few of my colleagues in literature, notably Irving Fineman and Ben Belitt, had spent some time at Yaddo, periods of work when Irving was writing one of his novels, and Ben completing his first volume of poems, *The Five-Fold Mesh*. It was only an hour's drive from Bennington to Saratoga Springs, not far from Albany, New York. Then, some years later, during my first year of teaching at the University of Chicago, I planned to return to New England for the summer months, longed to do so in fact, to continue work on some writing I was doing. I applied to Yaddo, almost New England, for July and August, and was accepted by the Foundation.

The regimen followed at Yaddo suited me perfectly. The opulence and spaciousness of the room in which I wrote never ceased to delight me each morning I settled down for work after breakfast. Outside of my rooms, the mansion and all parts of the large estate, and the other guests, twenty-five of them, engaged in writing or painting or composing, formed a world in itself that I became familiar with at the end of the afternoon and at dinner when work stopped.

For all of us, I think, Yaddo represented freedom to work. If we wished to write steadily in solitude, there would be no interruptions between eight-thirty in the morning and four in the afternoon: no telephone calls allowed, no visit from another guest. We saw one another at breakfast, but that was usually a quiet meal with little talk. After breakfast each of us picked up a lunch pail (a sandwich or two, a piece of fruit and a thermos of coffee or milk) which we carried to our quarters: a studio, a bedroom, and a bath. We ate lunch whenever we wished, and alone. At four I took a walk, usually into Saratoga, to see people on sidewalks and visit a few stores. Then a bath, and dinner at one of the tables in the dining room where often the talk was very good. There was more interesting talk with painters than with writers, I soon discovered. Writers seemed to be worried about words, speech, expression of ideas because that had been their concern through the day. They tended to be more taciturn and less relaxed than the painters. Through my several periods of work at Yaddo, I encountered very few writers and painters who were teachers like me, and I grew to admire the nonteachers for their resoluteness, the purity of the vocation which they carried out, often with financial difficulty. We were all joined in an eagerness—it was almost a morbid avidity—to work long hours and thus profit from the weeks at Yaddo, free from household cares and other time-consuming duties. We were released from all such cares and were being tested in our worthiness or unworthiness in claiming to be creative writers or composers.

My case was more acute than others, because I was engaged in writing a book of literary criticism, and the other writers were either poets or novelists. Although I firmly believed in the creativity of criticism, I felt inferior to the poets and novelists, to the painters and sculptors and composers. I was writing a book based on other books while they were creating from the imagination and from their personal experiences and reactions. These feelings I had my first summer at Yaddo, but they diminished through the years as I began to understand that criticism too draws upon the personality of the critic, and that a novelist draws upon other novelists in ways very similar to the practice of a critic. No work of art is positively unique.

July first, 1946: the beginning of my first visit. I arrived by bus from Boston, and by taxi from the bus station in Saratoga. Mrs. Elizabeth Ames, the director of Yaddo, had sent me information about ways to reach the estate, which included even the name of the preferred taxi company. Clifford Wright helped me to my suite of rooms called "the den." I learned later that Clifford was a resident painter and worked half-time as an assistant in the office. From the drab-looking office we walked into the impressive hallway of the mansion, passed a fountain, and went up a wide, red-carpeted staircase to a corridor ending in a door that bore the word "den." Clifford was enjoying his role of guide and knew I would be amazed by the size and opulence of the den as he opened the door and showed me what were to be my quarters for two months. It was a very large room with generous bay windows that ran the length of the room. Under the bay windows curved a continuous seat or bench with attached pillows, wide enough for sleeping if one wanted to stretch out there and watch the sky or the stars. Close by the windows at the farther end was a comfortable-looking chaise longue. I knew what it was, but this was the first I had seen in real life, and I immediately imagined myself reading there in the afternoons, with the light from the bay windows coming over my right shoulder. Then, exactly in the middle of the room, stood a huge desk—the largest I had ever seen, to say nothing of ever having used, long enough and wide enough for ample writing space, a few dictionaries, a few books, note-books and paper, and folders that would be close at hand. The chair behind the desk was as massive as the desk itself. At one end of the desk a typewriter table appeared ready for use, with a mat and a chair. High up on the other wall, opposite the bay window, a line of casement windows provided light for the desk. A long shelf under the casement windows supported two objects to which I was to become attached: a small marble bust of Brutus and a virginal (a small, spinetlike instrument popular in the sixteenth and seventeenth centuries) which I soon discovered was not in good repair.

In a glance, and Clifford confirmed this, I could see that my den jutted out from the mansion itself. Under it was a carriage drive, with nothing above it. A heavy door, furnished with a gigantic lock and bolt, which Clifford helped me push open, turned out to be a sort of secret entrance, for there was a vine-covered gray stone stairway going down to a spot in the garden just beyond the driveway. "Legend has it," Clifford confided, almost in a whisper, "that Mr. Trask, original owner of Yaddo, used this den as a hideout, as escape from the formal life of the mansion, and the outside secret stairway was used by special lady friends." Perhaps only a rumor, the story seemed appropriate, and I imagined not Mr. Trask living in the den but my writing predecessors in their creative work and extracurricular activity.

The bedroom, attached to the den, was in another style: ascetic, with a brass bed, a bed table and lamp, and a chest of drawers for clothes. Beyond it, a large bathroom was to be shared with a fellow writer occupying the room opposite my bedroom. He would use his small bedroom only for sleeping, and do his writing in a studio in the woods! There was no shower, but a gigantic bathtub, and since the water in Saratoga was "hard," a special soap was provided.

Half museum, half studio, the den in which I was to live three other summers after the first summer, was so unlike any other room where I had lived and worked, that I worried at first that I might not adjust to its bigness and theatricality. Could I forget it as I worked in it? Would I be tempted just to live in it, and not write? It was such an overpowering room that my mind might be overtaken with one fantasy after another. My fears were groundless. The morning hours went well. They were the hours I spent in writing and re-writing at the desk. The absorbing subject I was working on—Rimbaud—was such that the room dissolved and I saw only the texts of *Les Illuminations*. They became reality for me, and the den became an unreal setting. During the afternoon hours when I typed some of the pages or letters, and used the chaise longue for reading, I enjoyed looking at the overflowing reality of that room, and imagined it belonging to some Italian villa with seventeen bedrooms containing uncles and aunts, parents and cousins, and even grandparents.

On that first day, by the time I had unpacked my bags of clothes and my bag of books and notebooks, it was too late to pay a visit to Mrs. Ames. I would perhaps see her at dinner and ask when I might call. Ten minutes before dinner I left my room and went down the wide, red-carpeted staircase that put me in the center of a spacious area—an atrium almost, with the fountain at one end and open glass doors at the other end leading to the porch and the distant rose garden. There were several people grouped around a lady seated in an arm-chair: obviously Mrs. Ames. In a glance I could see, opposite her chair, a large carved bishop's throne, or furniture that looked ecclesiastical, and beside it on the wall a mosaic representing a bird rising from flames—the phoenix, I supposed. Mrs. Ames greeted me cordially, with a few questions about my journey, and an invitation to drop by her house after dinner. Then she said, "Introduce yourself to the others."

As I moved from group to group, I heard several times the name "Truman." I seemed to be interrupting conversations about . . . could it be President Truman? Could he have been here at Yaddo? When I finally asked the question, there was laughter, and I was informed they were talking about Truman Capote, a young writer who had just left Yaddo after spending a few weeks there. He had not published anything as yet, but the committee that read submitted work of unpublished writers believed he showed promise. Truman Capote, during his Yaddo life, had had the habit of curling up in the bishop's throne and falling asleep there. At that moment we were all standing in front of that throne, and the absent Truman had been evoked.

When a maid opened the dining room doors, all the guests had gathered—about twenty-five, I estimated—and we went into a spacious dining hall with a few large tables and a few smaller ones. John Malcolm Brinnin, whom I had met a few years earlier at Bennington and whom I was pleased to see again, invited me to join him and Clifford Wright at one of the smaller tables. They were admirable initiators to life at Yaddo, to bits of information about the past and the present, to the habits and behavior of the guests. In a jocular fashion, and in great friendliness, they put me at ease, guided me around the serving tables, and urged me to enjoy the fresh salad which had come from the Yaddo garden. I could see at that first meal that the guests were well-fed, and I knew already they were well-housed.

After dinner John and Clifford walked outside with me to point out some of the paths and studios, and then showed me the house of Elizabeth Ames where I was expected. The door opened as I approached it and, for a second time, Mrs. Ames welcomed me to Yaddo. Tall, stately, with an expression of peacefulness and contentment on her face, she spoke with combined gentleness and authority. She did indeed represent Yaddo. She had been its director since it opened to the first guests in the 1920s. I knew little of the history of the estate, and she informed me with precision and with obvious pride in Yaddo and her position there of the origins of the corporation of Spencer and Katrina Trask who had left Yaddo, as a memorial to their two young children, to be used as it was actually being used. In most of Elizabeth's conversation there were allusions to the history of Yaddo, but her principal interest seemed to be in individual writers who had been there and with whom she had established a friendly and at times a sentimental relationship. The bond of sentiment was the writer's appreciation of Yaddo and the successful way in which he or she worked there. Yaddo has housed many of the best-known American writers and composers. The world's recognition of books and musical works, some of which were created at Yaddo, were in the eyes of Elizabeth justification for maintaining the community.

Her principal advice on that first meeting was not to push myself at the beginning, not to drive myself to work, but to become accustomed to the setting, to the pattern of the day, and thus thwart any overeagerness. It was sound advice. How could she know me that well, I wondered, or is this standard advice she gives to every new guest? Even that first evening Elizabeth touched deftly, briefly, on a few stories concerning guests of previous years in order to underscore what should be my attitude toward work during the first days at Yaddo. As time went on that first summer, and on other visits through the years, Elizabeth's stories, usually told at dinner when several guests would be attentive, were longer and were told with sympathy and wit.

Even if I was familiar with the stories, I enjoyed hearing them again, not because of the stories but because of the way in which she told them to newcomers. She was at those moments the head of the household, knowledgeable about the years of Yaddo, the legends, the happenings, the names, and the anecdotes associated with some of the names. Elizabeth was the source of all knowledge, and she distributed it, as she saw fit, with an almost queenly condescension. In the 1960s people began to urge her to write her memoirs and thus perpetuate the stories she told us. Soon Elizabeth announced that she was writing her memoirs, but I doubt if she ever did. They were fluent, graphic stories told to new and old guests at the dinner table in the mansion or in her living room. But as I remember them now, no character emerged clearly. Elizabeth observed incoherences as well as natural sequences of a person. She had not learned the writer's task—to take one thing, one word, and let it stand for twenty. The last time I heard some of the stories—not long before her death—my interest was suffocated under a plethora of words.

Her life became Yaddo's. The guests and members of the staff had lives and activities away from Yaddo. Elizabeth did not. Easier on men than on women, she could be harsh on those who misbehaved or appeared disloyal to the spirit of Yaddo. To those guests who returned frequently, who worked well, and who were known in their specialty, she became a good friend but limited her friendship to the boundaries of the estate, to the highway outside the gate, to the racetrack that bordered the estate, to Saratoga as the extreme limit. Yaddo was an entire world in itself. No one needed to be elsewhere, and it behooved us all to forget what went on elsewhere. She was the lord-lady and we were vassals. An example of feudalism in New York state.

Many years later, in the eighties when I read a remarkable novel by Iris Murdoch, *The Unicorn*, I recognized Elizabeth Ames in the leading character. Hannah is the mistress of a castle set in a wild county in Northern England, close to a dangerous bog. She is beautiful and mysterious. Her past is never fully revealed. She is loved, revered, and feared by those who live with her in the castle. She is the imprisoned lady. From time to time efforts are made to help her escape, but they end disastrously. Neither Hannah nor Elizabeth wanted to escape. The prison of each was the world in which she was prisoner and jailer.

After the first two weeks of that early visit, Henri Cartier-Bresson came to work for a brief time at Yaddo. I had seen examples of his photographer's art and wondered if he was interested in making a photographic study of Yaddo. He was accompanied by his Javanese wife, a dancer who was visible very seldom, even at dinner, and who, according to rumor, practiced her dance exercises in their suite in the mansion. John Brinnin introduced me to Cartier-Bresson after dinner the first evening and suggested that I show the photographer the rose garden.

It was the first hour at Yaddo when I spoke French with someone, and when I served in a modest way as a guide to a newcomer. I was curious to learn how Cartier-Bresson planned to use Yaddo in the practice of his art. The project in which he was engaged was already well under way. He was accumulating a series of candid camera shots of lovers unaware that they were being photographed: two lovers kissing as they stood under a bridge, for example, or a pair holding hands as they sat on a park bench. They were scenes from more than one country, in deserted places and in subways, night scenes and day scenes. His literary collaborator was to be John Malcolm Brinnin, whom he had asked to compose a few lines to accompany each picture. They could work together at Yaddo, and Henri could continue using Saratoga and the racetrack, the rose garden, the bars on Main Street, the bus station, as possible sites of revelations of passion.

This creative enterprise was very real for both photographer and poet—a book did appear later—and for me, as I listened to it being discussed, was symbolic of this life so centrally concerned with the creation of art. I often wondered about the variety of projects being pursued close by me, in the mansion, in west house, in the studios. And that led me to wonder about what I was writing that summer of 1946, in the fashion of that year, and during subsequent periods of work at Yaddo. Would it, in five or ten years, look as dowdy and dull as any other fashion that has served its time?

On my return to Chicago that fall of 1946, I met, largely because of Yaddo, Morton Dauwen Zabel who had recently joined the English department at the University of Chicago after teaching many years at Loyola. He was a fervent Chicagoan, a brilliant literary critic, and a member of the board of Yaddo. We often met for dinner and concerts that year. Morton himself was an excellent pianist. Then, on my second visit to Yaddo, in the summer of 1949, he was there for two weeks. It was really a vacation respite for him, a few days of relaxation when he enjoyed renewing his contact with Yaddo for which he worked hard in serving on various committees. I was moved by his devotion to the place, by his loyalty to Elizabeth Ames, by the courtesy and interest he showed to every writer and artist with whom he spoke at dinner, or after dinner in the large music room where several of us used to listen to records.

Morton was the most erudite teacher and critic I have known, particularly during the days when we were together at Yaddo. I marveled at his memory for details and facts, for bibliography and dates, for titles and obscure references. I marveled too at the incisiveness of his mind, his judgments and standards, his underlying love for literature. Behind the thick lenses of his glasses his blue eyes sparkled whenever arguments began, whenever a controversy started up, and he defeated us all with his ever-present knowledge of whatever subject was being discussed.

Soon after my arrival that summer, I sat down at dinner one evening with a poet whose work I was just beginning to read with admiration: Elizabeth Bishop. Young, beautiful, disarmingly and sincerely modest, she delighted me with her quick flashes of wit—they too were modest—as we spoke of living at Yaddo and trying to work there. She had been a guest for a fairly long time, and I was curious to learn how feasible that was—to live for several months away from one's normal mode of existence. I had already begun wondering about how suitable Yaddo was for poets who presumably worked more intensively and more briefly each day than writers engaged in longer works of prose. Elizabeth explained some of the devices she created to interrupt the hard work and relax, which would lead her back into the actual writing. She was so averse by nature to anything dogmatic or arbitrary that her thoughts were expressed in quasi-whimsical terms. One had to sense their underlying seriousness.

Among other "devices," she mentioned visits to various stores in Saratoga, notably Woolworth's, and listening to colloquial phrases or words that might be the start of a line of poetry or the idea of a poem. Blowing soap bubbles from the balcony of her room was a relaxing exercise, as she watched the bubbles catch the light of the sun and float down. Above all, easy pieces by Bach she played on her clavichord provided intervals between periods of labor. Elizabeth played some of those pieces for me (the ones written for Anna Magdalena Bach). Her clavichord, of small size, traveled with her in a conveniently fashioned box. Since I was the proud owner of a clavichord made by Dolmetsch in 1906 for Chickering, and since both of us were equally poor players, we discussed our repertoire—the easiest possible pieces of Couperin and Monteverdi.

Elizabeth's first book, *North and South*, had recently been published, and the most astute poetry critics had acclaimed its importance. After dinner one evening, on a walk through the woods, I told her how much I admired the sestina, "A miracle for breakfast." She looked at me a bit surprised, and said: "No one has seemed to realize it is a sestina." I told her then how at one time in a graduate course on Provençal, I had become almost an expert on the sestinas of Arnaud Daniel, the poet who is thought by some philologists to be the inventor of the sestina. I told her then, in total sincerity, that I thought "A miracle for breakfast" superior to those sestinas I had found in Eliot and Pound and Auden.

"I never worked longer or harder on any other poem, but I was happy all the time."

"Are the new poems you are working on here giving you that happiness?"

The answer Elizabeth gave me to that question I jotted down in my journal that very evening. It was not a direct answer, but it was far more than an answer. "In hoping to live days of greater happiness, I forget that days of less happiness are passing by."

Before I met Elizabeth again, on another visit to Yaddo, she had published her second volume of verse in which I found that magical poem, "Invitation to Miss Marianne Moore," that opens:

> From Brooklyn, over the Brooklyn Bridge,
> on this fine morning, please come flying.

It was to be my privilege in the fifties to cross Brooklyn Bridge and meet Marianne Moore, and speak with her about the poems of Elizabeth Bishop, about the woman writer, and especially the woman poet. In lesser women writers I had often felt, to my discomfort, an unnatural self-assertiveness, a vision either too feminine or too masculine. I learned, in reading the poems of Elizabeth Bishop and Marianne Moore, that a poem is a statement about objects, even divine objects. And then I discovered that the art of the poem relates the objects to each other. The poem makes a vision holding them in place. I learned that poems, as well as fiction, are based on life.

Women in literature, that is, the portraits of women in literature, was a theme Elizabeth and I discussed during those two summers at Yaddo. Once they were the almost exclusive creation of men, and then in England in the nineteenth century a woman's presence pleading for the rights of her sex was felt in George Eliot's *Middlemarch* and Charlotte Brontë's *Jane Eyre*. For such novelists, the sentence created by man was too loose, too heavy, too pompous. They created a woman's sentence which has been steadily refined until today when we have the woman's sentence of Virginia Woolf, Flannery O'Connor, and Eudora Welty that takes the natural shape of a woman's thought.

From the words I heard Elizabeth speak, as well as from her poems, I learned that there is no rest for the writer, whether poet or novelist or critic. A poem may come from other poems, or from the taste of a croissant, from the sound of a child crying, from the sight of a car speeding down the highway. The writer is constantly receiving impressions that sharpen his sensibility. Everything is made to serve his purpose —often in agony, as Flaubert recorded, and as Elizabeth once said to me at Yaddo, with more simplicity and modesty than Flaubert emphasized. Poets write their perceptions, and rewrite them, until the words correspond to their perceptions. And here I credit the final formulation to Flaubert: "le mot et l'idée sont consubstantiels."

In the early fifties—I believe it was 1951—my third period of work at Yaddo, still the summer vacation, coincided with a moment when Katherine

Anne Porter was a guest. I imagine that Miss Porter lived longer periods of time there than any other guest. Elizabeth Ames seemed proud of having her there, allowed her to dominate the scene and preside, not as director, but as goddess, as a mysterious figure appearing and disappearing, bestowing a smile or a word on a few of us. William Goyen was a devoted friend of Katherine Anne, and his bedroom that summer was opposite my den. I enjoyed his company and conversation. He insisted at one dinner that she allow me to join them. It was a delightful meal: Katherine Anne was in high spirits and I was captivated.

At one moment she actually asked me a question: "What do you do to relax at Yaddo?"

Glibly, too quickly, I replied, "I play Ping-Pong."

"Will you teach me?"

The first and only lesson was a disaster. Katherine Anne was unable to hold the paddle correctly or to make any decent connection with the ball. It went everywhere over the room, much to the delight and applause of the guests who began collecting. I swear she aimed directly at the ceiling rather than at the table. She wanted to beat me, not on the head, as I first thought she meant, but at the game, before I had introduced any remarks about counting or keeping score.

An innocent at games, Katherine Anne often played the role of innocent at the dinner table whenever reference was made to her stories. Her first collection, *Flowering Judas*, had by then become almost a classic, widely used in schools and colleges. The critics had begun analyzing and interpreting the stories, and whatever questions arose at Yaddo about her stories were always specific theories of this critic or that critic. Her comment was always the same: "I am just a storyteller, and I am puzzled by what those learned critics find in my stories." Such a remark puzzled me because more than most storytellers, Katherine Anne Porter was fully conscious of her characters and the symbolism of their actions and of such objects as a flowering judas tree. She played the game of innocent writer more skillfully than Ping-Pong.

I pondered over the difference between the beautiful lady seated at our table, witty, and even frivolous at times in her speech, and the serious, already celebrated writer. I knew that more than in her conversation, the text of her life was in the secret of those intact pages. What an outrage writing is! How relentlessly, as in the case of Katherine Anne Porter, does it classify, prune, and reassemble the writer's life!

During that summer at Yaddo I wanted to ask Katherine Anne one question which I never had had the courage to ask, because I knew she would give me a cutting, deadly answer. The question was, "For whom do you write? There must be some patron, some desirable being you wish to please." If she had allowed me to get that far with my question, I would have continued by reminding her that Shakespeare had the playhouse public he wrote for, and Racine had a mistress. I imagine Henry James despised his vast public. Patron-finding! What a test for any author! If you find the patron, then you know how to write. I imagined Katherine Anne turning on me then and asking, with scorn in her voice, the same question: "Whom do you write for? Who is your patron?" I would have been ready for the question, and I would have said: "I write for undergraduates, to share Rimbaud with them, and at great risks. When I write for such a patron, I know he is immune from shock. Indecency no longer plagues me."

In August of that summer, another short-story writer came to Yaddo (much younger than Katherine Anne who had already left), who quickly became for me a walking companion at four o'clock each afternoon. J. F. Powers, called Jim, came from Minnesota. His first published story had appeared in *Accent* a few years earlier, in the same issue with my first published essay. Our first exchange of words was an expression of gratitude to the two cordial editors of *Accent*, published by the University of Illinois. Jim was a tall, handsome, athletic-looking man who, at his first dinner at Yaddo, a Saturday, asked me where the Catholic church was in town. I told him the nearer one (there are two in Saratoga) was the Paulist Church, and we walked there the next morning. It was the first of our many walks.

I was familiar with his stories, collected under the title *Prince of Darkness*, with their Irish parish priests in towns of Minnesota, with their concern over changing mores in Catholicism and the underlying permanent ones.

We spoke of many matters during those walks, when I enjoyed Jim's open mind, his warm spirit, and the awe with which he gave himself to his writing. We spoke of Yaddo, naturally, and of the effect we thought the place might have on our writing, of the fate of the contemporary writer whose work was produced with infinite pains, and of the making of a critic. Jim often returned to this subject of the critic, since I was there, close at hand, and trying hard to be one. Again that summer I was the only guest writing a critical work, and making every effort to keep my head not too far below the heads of the novelists and poets and short-story writers.

I did confess to Jim, when he pummelled me with questions, that a great critic is the rarest of beings because it is hard for a critic to remain where he should remain, in the full flood of creative activity. I tried to point out, not facetiously, that the fate of all the writers at Yaddo depended on the critics, on attention being paid to their publications, be it adverse or favorable. Without critical attention the work will disappear. When Jim asked, "What goes into the making of a critic?" I answered without hesitation, "A generous nature and a society sufficiently ripe to listen to a critic's assessment." The critic is the man among us who pits his century against another. He will ask: "Our century has industry, but is it an age of sustained effort in the writer? Will it have a masterpiece, will it have its *Madame Bovary*, its *Pride and Prejudice*?" He may easily point out that D. H. Lawrence has moments of greatness, but also hours of monotony. He is the man who ultimately assigns the prizes to *Ulysses* and *Remembrance of Things Past*.

The days of August that summer passed too quickly. Each morning I worked on Rimbaud's *Une saison en enfer*, and had come to the last section that opens with the words,

"L'automne déjà!"

With that fragment of a text very securely in me, I met Jim one afternoon at our usual spot for our walk. The colors were changing in the leaves. The dark rich reds and yellows of the fall flowers seemed stronger to me than ever, and to myself, but aloud, as we began our walk, I mumbled: "L'automne déjà!" Jim stopped and looked at me. "What a beautiful rhythm in those words! Say that again."

I was startled because I had not recited them in any direct way to him. But I did repeat the phrase: "L'automne déjà." Then Jim tried it himself, still marveling at the sound. "Once more," he said, and once more I spoke the phrase, and paid more attention than I had before to the rhythm of the two words. We continued our autumn walk, and on all subsequent walks we recited the Rimbaud phrase as the signs of autumn grew more and more evident. I remember trying to add to our modest litany the phrase: *O saisons! ô châteaux!* and explain what I thought they meant, but it did not have for Jim as novel an intonation as *l'automne déjà*.

During the two Augusts I was there in the 1960s, my cousin Polly Hanson, who worked on the staff at Yaddo, had purchased, as soon as they were available, tickets for the New York City Ballet—the Balanchine–Lincoln Kirstein company—that performed two weeks at Saratoga and attracted large audiences. Like other Yaddo guests, we watched the stories of those ballets unfold in their strange, miraculous stylization. We relaxed from practice of the craft that had held us through the day. Inevitably I contrasted in my mind the achieved art of performance on the Saratoga stage with that art in the making which I labored on in my "den," or hoped would turn into some form of art. I was still writing in notebooks paragraphs that might never appear in a book. Would Time take them into his hands, rewrite the scrawls, and put them into something suitable, something that I could call "useful"?

During the mornings I kept my eye on a certain poem of Mallarmé, or on a figure of speech in a Mallarmé sonnet, and tried to write what I saw, what I heard as I read the stanza aloud. I was not unlike one of my painter companions at Yaddo who kept his eye on a naked figure in his studio, or on a dish of lemons, and copied it. That metaphor I studied moved about, from stanza to stanza, from poem to poem. It changed, and yet it was the same. During those evenings at ballet, I kept my eye on the ballerina or on a group of dancers who never stayed in one spot. They moved constantly. They changed from one form into another, as they told a story that was quite easy to follow.

Their miraculous control of the body I watched in the evenings was like a figure of speech that helped keep me steady as I studied Mallarmé's *Toast funèbre* each morning. The ballet was about more than one person, about more than one time. It taught me that I had to learn to seize on more than one poem, one metaphor, one stanza at a time. I read with renewed wonderment the pages that Mallarmé had written on dance, on the music-drama of Wagner, on the mass, on the meaning of "performances." They helped me with my study of images in the poems and they helped me every evening at the ballet, as I followed those explosions of bodies that gave form to the most persistent human sentiments.

Those two summers had a great "purity" about them, thanks to the Mallarmé mornings and the ballet programs in the evenings. I say "purity" because I resolutely moved away from poetic theory to a study of the poems themselves, and away from plays with their monologues and dialogues to speechless dance. And those were the summers when I met Violette Verdy on a few occasions. She was the ballerina I enjoyed most watching on the stage. She had come to Yaddo on previous summers, invited by some of the guests, and had become a good friend of cousin Pauline. An intellectual ballerina. We had very few conversations—the three of us—usually after a performance, in an ice cream parlor. She spoke once of dancers descending from other dancers, as families descend from families. Living dancers resemble their forebears. And I thought instantly of how Mallarmé resembles Maurice Scève.

It was the same person who sat before an ice cream soda and who, forty minutes earlier, had danced her role in *Jewels* with impeccable skill and beauty. How does one explain such a metamorphosis? We spoke of Paris, of problems of the day—simple and complex problems—which would disappear from my mind when she danced the next evening. And I thought of Mallarmé writing some of his poems through the Franco-Prussian War without a mention of the war, and of Jane Austen living through the Napoleonic Wars and never referring to them in her writing. Can it be the same for a writer today? Yes, I believe it can, despite television that shows us in the evening a battle that raged somewhere in the world a few hours earlier.

Mallarmé had died sixty years ago, and yet he was more real for me than the Yaddo guests I spoke with at dinner. Yes, more real than Elizabeth Bishop, Katherine Anne Porter, J. F. Powers, and the dancer Violette Verdy. Often the living blind us to our clear vision of human life.

There were a few symphony concerts also those summers, after which Ned Rorem often joined Pauline and me for an ice cream treat. Although I have seen him in other places—Chapel Hill and New York—I associate Ned Rorem with Yaddo where our visits often coincided, and where I learned to rely on him and his brilliant conversation to bring me back (if I had strayed) into the center of French thought and art, and especially into linguistic problems: French grammar, vocabulary, idioms. His mind moved ceaselessly between the correct use of a French idiom and such glorious names as Poulenc, Boulez, Marie-Laure de Noailles, Jean Cocteau. The Yaddo collection of records in the music room had many of his songs. The poems he chose were as admirable as the music he composed for them—art songs in the great tradition. As I listened to them, I moved back in time to the recitals of Povla Frijsh I had attended so avidly as an adolescent in Jordan Hall, Boston, and I tried to imagine, nostalgically, how the Danish soprano would have interpreted Ned's songs.

When together at Yaddo, we spoke very seldom of music. He worked hard in his studio, and when out of it he seemed to prefer to talk of other matters, and especially of his loving concern with things French. It was not an effort on Ned's part to indulge me in what I too loved best, but something closer to testing me. In a graceful, alluring way he was a pedagogue who with pointed questions, not innocently asked, revealed in his friend weaknesses in knowledge and understanding. At times his questions, to the pedagogue's satisfaction, turned up information he quickly assimilated.

There was no confusion, no blur in Ned's mind. His unconsciousness, his

under-mind worked daily at top speed (and still does). At one moment he
would doubt me — that was visible on his face — and then, if by chance, if by a
miracle, I knew the answer, and could prove it, he would smile, and I was back
in his favor, momentarily. His big questions were usually in the form of "How
does one learn one's art? How does one live by one's art?" Then abstract
speculations would follow, adorned with references to the science of language.
An autodidact in a way, he learned a great deal from conversations with the
famous and less famous. Multiple influences of people and places are recorded
in his mind, and now some of them appear in the volumes of memoirs he
has published.

My last two visits at Yaddo were winter visits—the month of January,
late sixties and early seventies—and these I enjoyed more than Saratoga in
summertime. The mansion was closed then, and I was assigned to West House,
room one, a combined bedroom and study. From my window I could see
Elizabeth's house, and each morning I watched her walk down the shoveled
path—to arrive first for breakfast served in a dining room over the garage. We
were more closed-in during the winter. There were only eight or ten guests
who, like me, enjoyed the winter scenes outside and the inducement to work
more steadily inside, and to know one another more easily at dinnertime when
all sat around one table.

On the first of those January visits, Marc Blitzstein replaced Ned as the
composer in our group. His conversation was equally brilliant, and different
from Ned's in that Marc asked few questions and told more stories than Ned
did. But the two men had a similar love for France and a sensitive knowledge
of things French. Ned's world centered on French aristocracy (*le comte de
Noailles*, who gave a million francs to Cocteau and Buñuel to help them make
their first films), and Marc's world centered on the theater with its glamorous
and intemperate cast of characters. With Marc we moved back and forth
between Paris and New York, between Jean Giraudoux and Lillian Hellman.

His was a mind trained on the arts, not only music but painting and literature, and a mind cultivated on worldliness that had never been tricked by mere
worldliness. I listened avidly to the speech of Marc Blitzstein, to whatever he
might say to the small group that gathered for drinks before dinner in West
House, and to the stories he might tell during dinner in the winter dining
room, and to the continuous talk after dinner in the small library beside the
dining room. He spoke as if he had been silent for too long during the work-
day hours. He spoke with wit and perceptiveness as if he had rehearsed his
thoughts and stories. Wit he had, but no trace of malice. His words that

entertained and delighted all of us were slightly contradicted by the expression of sadness that often passed over his face. A year later I grieved for Marc when I read of his death in the *New York Times*.

A strong memory remains in me from the last January I spent at Yaddo. It was the seventies, a decade ago, and I was working—at least part of the time—on revising and enlarging an autobiographical book, *Pantomime*, which I wanted to rename *Journal of Rehearsals*, and thus retain a reminiscence of the clown and the actor who seem to be part of my teacher's makeup. At the first dinner that January I was delighted to meet Galway Kinnell, some of whose work I knew: his own poems and his translations of Villon and Yves Bonnefoy. He was stronger-looking than I had imagined him, quietly strong, unassuming because there was no need to assume any gesture or word not authentically his own.

After Eliot and Pound, the poets in English who had held me the most had begun to write about 1925: Auden, Spender, C. Day-Lewis, Louis MacNeice. Their books had been written under the influence of change. A world in change, in revolution: Germany, Russia, Italy, Spain. That January at Yaddo, when I reread poems of Galway, I realized clearly for the first time that he belonged to the new group of poets. The discord and bitterness in the poems and novels written between 1930 and 1950 were no longer apparent in the newer works. In the words I heard Galway speak and in his poems, there was no sniping at the bourgeois scapegoat. He articulated the new kind of community, of a few members of the community, where the mind was agile and respected and where the body was given its due. The poet is more bare in Galway, closer to the French poets he admires and translates: fifteenth-century Villon and the contemporary Bonnefoy.

I observed and learned from Galway Kinnell, as I had learned a few years earlier from Elizabeth Bishop, that a poet's education is less definite than other forms of education. It is made up of reading, listening, talking, travel, leisure, of many things mixed together. Life and books are shaken up in him in right proportions. The novelist too, as well as the poet, has to be apart from others, so that his power of communication will grow. Somehow the simplicity of the Yaddo dining room, and the relaxed expression on Galway's face during those winter dinners, gave me the assurance that the memory of many studies and experiences was safe within him: the Elizabethans and Proust, his wife and his son.

During the day I worked on some attenuated chapters of my life that were for me sacred, lunatic connotations. At the end of each day, thanks to the Yaddo hospitality and the chance of talking with Galway Kinnell I was able to have some perspective on the project that held me through the day. I was able to see better into the dark passage from conception to work. The poems and the presence of Galway helped me to understand that my relations are not always toward people, but toward nature and destiny.

His technique had been learned early in his career, and at the time I met him he was the poet freed from the practice of technique. I moved to him gratefully, tired as I was of halfhearted attacks on bourgeois society. There was no compulsion to preach in his poems and in his conversation. Even in Auden there is a didactic, pedagogic tendency. Poetry is always ending and beginning again. Galway was the new voice for me that winter. The snow piled high outside, and the quiet thoughtfulness of the poet inside, convinced me once again that we live partly in a world that is dying and partly in a world struggling to be born. I had gone through that experience in studying Rimbaud and Mallarmé, and in the seventies I needed to realize it more completely. In my morning work that winter I was trying to write something a man remembers when he is alone. The memory of the heart is the absence of memory. It is memory springing from the chance of sensations.

On the Yaddo estate there are three bass ponds on three levels. A strong memory of those ponds still haunts me. It was August of my second or third visit when I had the habit of a late-afternoon walk that led me into the wilder parts of the property past the ponds. Usually I encountered no one. But one day, as I approached the third and highest pond, I heard voices and the sound of splashing water. Someone must be swimming, despite the signs forbidding such an act. As I turned a bend in the road, three fellows, naked, were emerging from the pond and trying playfully to grab the one towel that seemed to be available.

As I came closer, they called out: "Are you after us? Are you going to squeal on us?" I assured them I was neither a guard nor a squealer, and told them I too had often been tempted to take a swim on this habitual afternoon prowl of mine.

By that time I was certain they were jockeys from the nearby racetrack. Their bodies were so thin—gossamer threads would have described them— that they must have been submitted to a rigorous regimen. Yes, they were jockeys who came up from the south each August and rode the horses in the mornings around the practice tracks. And yes, they worried constantly about their weight. I learned they weighed themselves twice a day, and had been doing so almost all the years of their lives. They had literally grown up with horses being trained for racing. They spoke eloquently about ways by which to keep their weight at 110 pounds.

Then abruptly they turned to me and asked: "What do you do here?"

"I work in the big house, in the 'mansion,' as it is called."

"What do you mean by 'work'? Do you clean it?"

"No, I'm a guest. I am trying to write a book, and spend most of my day doing that."

They were frankly puzzled, even incredulous. "You spend all day writing? Is it a story for the movies? What is it about?"

The thin white bodies were by now half-dressed, and they had accepted me as an interloper like themselves. It was hard to explain what a book of criticism was. Writing a story would have made sense, perhaps, but writing a book about a story sounded silly, and even more silly when the story was in a foreign language.

I was beginning to squirm under their questions and trying to put my answers in terms they might recognize. "You worry about putting on a few pounds, and I worry about my adjectives, all the unnecessary words that I must cut out. If I make my book weigh less, then it may hit the mark and come in first."

"But why do you have to write about a French story, if that is what you do?"

"I studied French early, and became fascinated by the language, and then later by stories written in French. But you are right in a way to ask that question, which sometimes I ask myself. You see that sign over there warning you and me: "Trespassers will be prosecuted." It means that one day you may be caught swimming in this bass pond, and that one day I may be prosecuted for trespassing into a foreign territory." (Into Proust and Dante, I added under my breath.)

Briefly I described my typical day at Yaddo, and one of the fellows, the thinnest of the three, said, "It sounds like taking the veil."

We separated at that point, but we did meet on two other afternoons, and continued, half-seriously, half-jokingly, the comparison between pruning a page of prose already written and lopping off a pound of flesh by abstinence and swimming in a Yaddo fish pond.

Ever since those August days, I have kept in mind such phrases as *l'automne déjà*, and "the practice of prose, the practice of poetry, sounds like taking the veil." When the sign, "Trespassers will be prosecuted," flashes through my mind, I say to myself "Literature is not a private ground." And to the murky question, "What good is criticism?" I reply, "To tell us ultimately which books will last and which will perish."

9. The Basilisk

At the beginning of my fourth year of teaching at the University of Chicago, I found a furnished apartment on Woodlawn Avenue, near the campus, and settled there, relieved to find at last a place of my own. During my first three years at the university my good friends John and Nina Meyer had allowed me to rent their guest room and bath. There was a period of acute housing shortage following World War II. I had become a member of the Meyer family and was grateful to them for giving me shelter. But I had yearned for an apartment of my own and solitude when I needed it.

Work at the university had been strenuous and all-absorbing. I had been appointed principally to teach two sections of the third-year humanities course in the college. At the same time the graduate school had invited me to give each quarter a course in French literature. In preparing these new courses I learned to use my office in Wiebolt and the library. I had no home of my own and hence little chance of seeing new friends I would like to have seen.

"Humanities 3" represented in essence the university's belief in the "great" books, promulgated by President Robert Hutchins and Mortimer Adler. The reading list, carefully chosen by Richard McKeon and younger teachers trained by him, was composed of texts designed to teach a student how to talk about a literary text or a work of art. It represented, in a word, various approaches to the art of criticism. The first two texts in the course were the most carefully studied: Plato's *Phaedrus* and Aristotle's *Poetics*. They would be constantly referred to in the study of all the subsequent texts, such as Lessing's *Laocoön* and Kenneth Burke's analysis of Keats's "Ode on a Grecian Urn."

Each year I gave this course, and always in two sections, I became personally more involved with it, and in particular with the *Phaedrus*. On my own, and for my own pleasure and enlightenment, I read more and more widely in Plato, finding in his dialogues signs that he was the founder of all European philosophy and theology. By the time my fourth year began, in my newly found apartment, I was dividing my time between Plato and a new graduate course on Molière I had never taught previously.

The program delighted me and the students also, particularly the undergraduates who enrolled in "Humanities 3." My personal life was somewhat restricted. John and Nina Meyer remained my closest friends in Chicago. At the university I enjoyed the friendship of Morton Zabel, who took me on tours of the city he knew so well. We often attended concerts together with his sister Barbara. Two new friends, both poets and not connected with the university, Henry Rago and Hayden Carruth, were beginning to seek me out often, and they led me to stalwart supporters of *Poetry* magazine, notably Julia and Gus Bowe, and Mrs. Strobel, mother of the painter Joan Mitchell. With my new apartment I looked forward to seeing students more easily and more frequently.

As the fall session and the fall season began seriously in Chicago, an encounter took place which developed through the following months into an experience of importance for me. It had all the elements of a novel, and I grew to see myself as a character in such a work.

As I was leaving my last class one morning, in a hallway crowded with students coming and going from classrooms, a tall fellow approached me and said he wanted to speak to me briefly. I suggested that we go outside and that he walk along with me a few blocks down the midway. His courteous manner was soon mixed with arrogance and even insolence. It was an attitude of manliness and independence that I had noticed many times in my Chicago undergraduates. In New England such behavior would not be apparent in any of the colleges I knew. I was a bit put off by it in Seth, but I was also curious enough to suggest that he come that evening to my apartment where we might talk. That was what he obviously wished to do.

As soon as the fellow left me on the street, I regretted my invitation, and I regretted it all the more when I went into my quiet apartment with its neat piles of books and papers, with its notebooks on one corner of the large writing desk I used. Would all that be shattered by Seth's presence? I had been rash, too quick in giving in to his request for a talk "as soon as possible." My hope was that he might not come, and then I would be more reluctant to give in to a second request.

But at eight o'clock sharp the doorbell rang and I pressed the button to open the front door downstairs. He came into the room so deliberately that he seemed to be taking possession of it. When he sat down and the conversation began, I soon realized that Seth was going to expound his own thoughts and problems more than question me about mine. His handsome face with its Semitic features contrasted with his Chicagoan brashness. In the space of just a few minutes he passed from mood to mood. His eyes were outraged when he attacked the universe for not giving him what he wanted, and then, without going through any intermediary stage, his eyes smiled as if to pay up for any initial hostility. But I knew that no smile was really tolerant for him.

"What makes you click right now in your life, professor? What are you high on?"

The question was a test and I decided to answer it forthrightly.

"My brain this year is impaled on a few Greek writers, on one in particular —Plato. I am just the shell of a man looking for a sky of brightness."

"What does all that mean?"

"It means, I suppose, that I am a lover of knowledge."

"Sounds queer."

"I suppose it is. Well, Seth, what turns *you* on? What is your passion?"

"Mine is glory, or fame, but I don't know which kind. I keep thinking that some morning I'll wake up with glory beginning to tremble in me as if it were some fever. That's why I've looked you up. Some of your students told me you're pretty keen on the glory of writers. When it comes to me, I'll take it to the window and fly off from there into the air. Glory means to me being high above the world."

"You know the story of Icarus, don't you?"

"Sure I do. There you go again. Another Greek!"

"I don't know too much about the air, but perhaps I can teach you how to walk in the sunlight without flying up to the sun. There are trees to walk under, even here in Chicago. We may even find some plane trees under which to walk."

The allusion had slipped out before I realized it. But it was lost immediately. Seth had not sensed the intrusion from the Greek world. He had stretched out on the couch and slipped off his tie. The talk was tiring him. After appearing strong and forceful, he abruptly changed. All color left his face. His body seemed abandoned as he lay there. No age was marked on him. The effort of speaking and saying something meaningful had exhausted him. When he left, soon after that moment of fatigue, I watched my room resume its proportions of quiet and order. On getting into bed, tired myself by then, I thought of Seth as a basilisk under leaves, his two eyes opened and gleaming from the metal-like carapace.

The next morning, a Saturday, the sky was gray. I went out onto the terrace where the wind lashed around me accumulating all smells. They were all the winds of the dying year. I felt far away from the land of my Greeks, but it was a good day for work, and I corrected a set of papers, prepared a class, and then opened the dialogue I was studying. I was soon lost in the purity of that Socratic world.

In the middle of the morning I heard a step on the stairs and then a gentle knock on my door. It was not Seth standing there, but a girl resembling Seth.

"I see you recognize me," she said. "I am Judith, Seth's only sister. We are very close and very much alike. He tells me everything, so I know already that you are a lover of knowledge. He even told me about your referring to a plane tree and a walk in the sun."

This very attractive girl had Seth's eyes. She was less tall than her brother and her hair and skin were darker.

"You are younger than Seth?" I asked.

"Yes, I am eighteen and he is twenty-one. You know many more things than we do."

By this time she had come into the room and had gone to the French doors at the porch. There she turned around and asked me an unexpected question.

"What did the Greeks teach about the soul?"

"They taught that the soul is immortal because it is always in motion like a bird."

We both turned to the light from the porch as if to see birds in the sky. There were none that morning.

"If there were birds in the sky, could you tell the future by them?"

"So, Judith, you know about augury. . . . Please tell me why you came this morning."

I asked the question that abruptly because there seemed to be no tension in her, only warmth and delicacy and a slight degree of aloofness.

"Seth did not send me here, as you might have supposed. He hates you this morning because you were friendly to him last night. You see, he never be-lieves anyone will continue being his friend. I came here this morning hoping that I could convince you to come by our house this evening. It would be a wonderful surprise for him. He and I are very much alike except for his violence. Please come and teach him a lesson on friendship."

Without too much hesitation I accepted this girl's invitation. I was curious to see the brother and sister together in the same room, although just a few minutes earlier I had felt relieved that Seth had moved out of my life. His moodiness and irrational whims had tired me the night before. But Judith had changed my resolve not to see him again. She was Seth without his tantrums and hates. She had a girl's gentleness. I wondered how well she understood her brother.

Their address was off 43rd Street, just a few I.C. stations down from 57th and closer to the Loop. The night was cold. The wind seemed to be hurling itself in a dull fury. When I reached the apartment house I rang the bell three times as Judith had told me to do. The brother and sister and their mother lived on the top floor. As I climbed the stairs, I saw the door was opened and a young girl stood there. It was Judith looking like a mere child.

"Seth doesn't know you are coming, and mother is out tonight."

We had been talking quietly just a few minutes when the door of the room was flung open and Seth was on us.

"What the hell! The reader of the Greeks himself." And then to Judith he said: "You worked it, didn't you, you sly thing?"

There was a first brief wave of hostility toward me, which soon became banter. And then the banter turned into insistent strident speech. I listened and Judith listened too, and to myself I recited the line: "Your love of discourse, Phaedrus, is superhuman." That sentence recalled was all I needed to send me into a world of sunlight and river coolness.

At one point when Judith came into the room bearing a tray of drinks, she led the way with the talk and Seth quieted down. It was then I realized the whole range of desire in me. Seth and I were joined in desiring this girl. My attraction to Seth had reached its full power in my attraction to the sister part of Seth. But he too was caught in the same kind of lyric trance where I was held. This was no mere range of desire —it was a full range of folly.

Suddenly, as if to break the spell, Seth stood up and yelled an order at me.

"We're taking the 9:37 I.C. to town. This is on me. Come on, move ass."

I played the game of docility, eager to break the experience of what I supposed was a kind of epiphany. We walked fast to the station and reached the platform just as the train slowed down and stopped: 9:37 on the dot. We stepped into one of the lighted coaches. It was a fast train, a ghost train with almost no passengers. When we reached Randolph Street Station, Seth was speaking volubly, deliriously, in his role of omniscient leader. The night had set him free.

"You are going to see and hear something that will revolutionize you. You won't recognize your Greeks tomorrow morning."

He dragged me down Randolph Street until we came to the Blue Note, a nightclub in the Loop. As I went down the stairs after Seth, I caught myself saying, *Tu, duca mio,* as if we were going into the earth, into an unknown circle of the underworld. The ticket seller looked to me like a Cerberus guardian. Seth argued with the hostess about the table. He wanted one near the band, in the front line of tables.

The band was blasting away in full fury. It was a shrill trumpeting of rapid notes, with perpetually the same rhythm and timbre. As I looked around me, the tables seemed to be islands in that space of hell, and the figures leaning over them seemed caught in some fated immobility. Seth winked at me with a patronizing smirk. When the piece ended, the applause was firm and appreciative. Seth gave me the explanation.

"That's Dixieland jazz, and the best there is. See the trumpeter in the center with the bow tie, the guy who looks sharp? That's Muggsy Spanier. He's been at this a long time. This music sends me."

After playing one more short number, the players left the platform. I turned to Seth.

"Why didn't we bring Judith? Was she too young?"

"You miss her already, do you? Just look at me. She and I are the same person. She exhausts me by being me. We survived all the hidden misery of childhood, but I'm not sure we'll survive our late adolescence. . . . Say, look over there by the wall. A new combo is coming."

Three black fellows were grouped beside the platform. When a fourth, heavier-set, carrying a bass viol, joined them, they all moved onto the stage. Seth was excited.

"This will be another kind of jazz. Bebop, they call it. It's softer, more dreamy than Dixieland. It's the closest thing we have today to the pipes of Pan. This combo is going to waft you to the Aegean Sea and back again to the Blue Note in the Chicago Loop."

At that moment a fifth musician appeared and made his way to the group. He was obviously the leader. Seth told me his name: Gene Ammons. He seemed to walk on air, impervious to everything around him, and especially indifferent to his audience, who clapped wildly. He raised his saxophone, licked the reed in his mouthpiece, threw back his head, and began to play. The others followed him, making a soft accompaniment to his sweet notes. "Sweet" was the word Seth used. It was suitable. Gene Ammons played in a world of dreams and nostalgia. He seemed to be in a trance. When he reached a high note, his body tensed. I was held by the contrast between Ammons's dark face and Seth's white death mask. I knew Seth must be going through a bad moment, and it broke as soon as Gene Ammons finished his first number.

"I'm sick of this hole. Let's get out of here!"

He threw a bill on the table and stalked out. This time I followed a fast-moving *duca*. I was both puzzled and worried. Why this sudden change, why this sudden loathing for the place to which he had wanted to go and had dragged me after him? Not until we got to the I.C. Station did Seth speak, and then, somewhat to my surprise, in a repentant mood.

"You'll get used to my fits. Feelings grow in me so fast, they choke me. Suddenly back there I felt jealous of Ammons, jealous of the way you listened to him. How I hate my loneliness! We'll get out at 43rd Street and walk down to the lake."

Seth was back into a mood of great gentleness and attentiveness. He no longer led. We walked side by side as we crossed a strip of rocks and boulders that had been dumped close to the lakefront. Our walk became an adventure with wildness. The sky was teeming and tearing along. It showed the terror of a moon running liquid-brilliant into an open patch of sky. We finally sat down on the top tier of rocks. It was a spot that Seth wanted to reach. He spoke of it as a favorite place for him and his sister.

"You can't hear the water tonight, but you can smell the wet rock. Judith and I used to come here for night swimming. At first, when we'd get into the water, we'd stay close together, bobbing up and down, holding onto the rocks. Then we'd swim out some distance to see the full line of the city from the lake itself."

Seth's face reflected the happiness he was telling me about. There was nothing of the basilisk in it, and yet the basilisk memory never left my mind, as I wondered about my attraction to these two creatures who always seemed to join into one at the end of each story Seth told me. When they turned back to the shore, he recounted, Judith would float on to Seth's back and he would tow her in. The two formed one body at such moments, and I ceased feeling jealous over either one.

We walked back to Seth's house that night and his quiet mood continued.

"What a tantrum I threw at the Blue Note! Why are we here together tonight? Your Greeks would have called it fate, I suppose. Wouldn't they say that the gods provoke such meetings and preside over such patterns as we formed tonight?"

Seth too was becoming obsessed with the Greeks. When we reached the front of his house, he pointed to the thin, straggly tree growing there.

"It's a hickory, I think. But let's call it a plane tree."

The wind blew hard at that moment and seemed to fold us together.

I was invited to dinner one evening especially to meet their mother. In various little ways I felt I was being inducted into the family. Judith wore a full black skirt and a white blouse. Her hair matched her skirt. When I asked her if she had prepared the dinner, she said no, that she was awkward in the kitchen, that her mother did the real cooking, and when it was ready to serve, she gave the meal over to Judith and pretended to be the grand lady hostess.

Shorter in stature than her two children, the mother was strikingly attractive, with hair styling that gave her an old-world appearance, and wearing a dress that might have come from Paris. She spoke to me graciously with a very slight foreign accent.

After the meal, and somewhat to my surprise, Seth pulled out the family album and showed me pictures of his father and of him and Judith at various ages. There was no picture of the mother. No need perhaps, because her features had been transposed into the faces of her two children. As he spoke of the pictures, Seth added a few anecdotes. One was about a plumber he had watched working one day in the kitchen when he was twelve. The plumber had made a prediction that Seth had never forgotten. With some pride he told us the prediction: "You will be famous some day, after committing a crime that no one would ever uncover." The photograph of Seth at twelve showed prominent shoulder muscles, and I thought: "That is where wings would begin if he were an angel. Perhaps he is that, an angel, or sphinx, or a tough guy." Out loud I told Seth that the plumber was his Tiresias.

At one point the mother asked me what I remembered best from my childhood, and I replied: "The fog along the Maine coast as it clung to the shore. It deformed all the familiar objects. I liked to walk in it."

"Here in Chicago," the mother replied, "we are too far away from the sea. There is never any fog like that from the lake."

Then Seth entered the conversation by saying, "There's no fog in Plato, is there?"

"No literal fog," I said, "but other themes compensate for it."

"Like what?"

"Like death. Philosophy is the study of death. Read the *Phaedo* where it says that true philosophers are always occupied in the practice of dying."

"That settles it." Seth was beaming. "I'm going to take up philosophy."

I made mention then of the philosopher seated on the bank of a river, in a plane tree grove that was beyond the city wall. But the conversation was interrupted by the mother suddenly leaving after calling for a taxi. I had felt tenseness in the room before this happened. It was obvious that Seth and Judith did not want their mother to leave. In just a few minutes Seth became furious, and, unable to restrain himself, he too left shortly after his mother.

Judith and I were alone. She was aware of my bewilderment and tried to reassure me.

"Seth is beyond our powers of help right now. There is no reason for you to follow after him. He will come back eventually, chastened by the night air."

We talked then, she and I, quietly, and I hoped she was beginning to feel how strongly attracted I was to her. She let me kiss her, but I realized that she was responding only to my loneliness. No one really existed for her but Seth. This thought was clear to me and it predicted my defeat. Was Seth in fact Orestes? Was he never tired of blood and wrongly throwing himself to risk? Was he trying to pierce through the dark and see the red eyes of Agamemnon? I had savored enough of the Atrides to last my lifetime.

I grew to enjoy the night walks Seth and I took beside Lake Michigan. For me it was the sea, and memories of my childhood came back to me forcibly. And yet that Chicago waterfront was entirely different from the ocean along the Maine coast. The ledges of rock housing the water glistened in their tiers as if by night they turned to marble. Seth's step was easy and relaxed. I admired the loose swing of his body and wished I could emulate him. The darkness rocked us.

I remember one night in particular when the moon had risen in that part of the sky over Gary where the horizon was always red from the light of the forges. The cold air smelled of the cornfields which lay to the west, of the dried stalks and the husks, of the hard earth turning black. Seth had become for me the debonair presence of night, and I recalled Plato's thought that philosophy should come from walking, that truth comes through vital concourse. And simultaneously with that thought, that other, almost daily question forced itself on me: was it the breath of the basilisk or a glance from its eyes that was mortal?

Then came, in the fatal unfolding of this drama, the final evening when Seth took full charge from the beginning. He led the way down the stairs, pushed

Judith and myself through the doorway into the cold night air, and hailed the first cab with such authority that he forced the driver into an unusual degree of obedience and submission. During the short ride he sat forward on his seat and maintained a steady chatter, partly nonsensical, partly directional. He was instructing Judith and me on what we were to expect from the evening.

The secrecy broke down when finally he had to explain that he was taking us to the home of the famous jazz pianist, Jimmy Yancey. Rapidly he provided a few facts as if he were conducting a tour.

Originally from New Orleans, Yancey had come to Chicago where he had worked as groundskeeper for the White Sox. He played the piano at night, and only at the top of his fame, ten years previously, had he given up his day work. Now he was old. He and his wife, Mama Yancey, a blues singer, no longer able to perform publicly, were penniless. On Saturday nights, friends and admirers came to their apartment in small groups where they spent the evening. The Yanceys played and sang, the friends listened, drank, danced, and left whatever they could afford in the way of money at the end of the evening.

When Seth made this announcement, only Judith was aware of its importance, but I did my best to join the enthusiasm by saying:

"I'm with you, Seth. It will be a second initiation tonight. Our visit to the Blue Note was my first."

It was a dismal, strange apartment. And it contained two distinct worlds. In the front room, where the piano was, were three or four groups of white people. Judith, Seth, and I formed one of those groups who throughout the evening stayed by ourselves. We were the tourists or listeners for whom Jimmy Yancey played and Mama Yancey sang. A small, intermediary room, quite empty, separated the front room from the back room where there were several black couples who danced while Yancey played. They stayed by themselves and manifested none of the almost fanatical enthusiasm of the front room visitors.

Yancey was standing by the upright piano when we entered the room. He was a thin man, slightly bent, whose black skin contrasted with the white-and-black striped silk shirt he wore. When he moved, he showed the litheness of a much younger man. He spoke jerkily with a rather gruff intonation. His wife always remained close beside him. She was shorter, her hair was gray, and her face was distorted by some accident or operation.

Seth quickly introduced his sister and took more time in introducing me, with the result that Yancey called me "the professor" and handed me an album of music.

"Go ahead, professor," he said. "It's my music. See my name on the cover. You choose whatever you want me to play, and I'll play it."

I sat down on the sofa facing the piano, turned over the pages of the album, chose a title and gave it to Yancey. Turning his back to all of us in the room, the pianist sat down on the bench and began to play. It was good playing and good jazz but had no relationship with the printed score. I tried to find it by turning the pages, but soon gave up and settled back on the sofa to enjoy the piece. Mama sat beside her husband and kept her head bowed.

Seth and Judith showed an almost religious attentiveness to the music. Two rooms away from where Jimmy Yancey played the piano, several black couples began dancing. The light was dim in that room, and a heavy curtain where the door would be was slightly drawn.

There was no particular preparation for an ending to the number. Jimmy simply stopped playing. His hands fell to his sides, but his body did not move. Neither did Mama move. There was applause from all those in the room and from the dancing couples in the other room. When it died down, Jimmy turned around with a smile on his face and asked me, "How did you like that, professor?"

"It was beautiful, Jimmy, and you played it like a master. But it wasn't the piece I asked for."

"Wasn't it now? Well, you just name another one, and I'll give it to you straight this time."

I chose another title. Jimmy again began to play, and again the notes he played were not those of the printed music. He probably was unable to read music, or else the titles of his own works were jumbled in his mind.

During the second improvisations, Seth began to drink. He forced a glass on Judith and me, and we pretended to join him. Our physical closeness to Jimmy and the excellence of his playing made the clinking of glasses and ice seem irreverent. Especially when Mama Yancey sang. She sang twice. They were "blues," tragic love stories which she performed with a shattering intensity. She stood close to her husband, who accompanied her. Her face, turned slightly up so that it caught the direct rays of the electric bulb, bore the full expression of the songs she sang. As her face took on the sad beauty of the songs, those of us who listened and watched forgot the distortion of her features.

When the second song was over—she called it "The Letter"—I asked her how she was able to feel the song so deeply and yet not allow her voice to break.

She answered proudly and simply: "A real singer never lets her voice break. She should bring tears to the eyes of all who listen, but never to her own eyes, professor. I've sung that song hundreds of times and only once did my voice break. But that one time was the biggest night of our careers. It was the night

Jimmy and I gave a concert in Carnegie Hall, New York. The place was packed. Such an audience! I was so keyed up that when I got to the end of that song, I couldn't stand it and my voice broke. I was so ashamed! Remember that, professor, you can't perform art and enjoy your feelings at the same time."

I looked around to see if Seth had heard those moving words from Mama Yancey. But Seth was then drinking his scotch straight and seemed in a happy, inattentive mood. Judith was trying to get him to dance with her as soon as Jimmy would begin to play. Her glance at me indicated that this was a simple stratagem to interrupt the drinking.

Jimmy did indeed go back to playing, and at that moment there was no need of forcing Seth. He was jubilant, almost raucously jubilant as he stood up. But as he led his sister in the rhythm of the music, his elation softened.

As I watched the brother and sister dance, I became convinced that this was the final scene of the strange story I had been living. It was time that my suffering stopped. I had been tortured long enough by the contradictory feelings of closeness to Seth and Judith, and total estrangement, total separation from them. Why delude myself any longer in believing that I could count in their lives, that I could lose myself in their history? This determination brought sadness to me. Judith and Seth had become sweet habits for my thoughts, for the hours in bed when I was not sleeping. But I knew at last that the silence and solitude of my life could not be peopled by these two.

I stood up then, interrupted the dancers, forced my way between them, and took Judith in my arms. Seth did not speak and did not change the expression on his face. He sank down into the nearest chair with an obvious feeling of relief as if his elation had worn off.

I did not speak to Judith but held her closely and danced without moving in very much space. I realized she was concerned about Seth, and I kept turning her around so that she could watch her brother.

When we sat down, there was no other couple dancing in the room. But in the second room beyond, the black couples still danced. The conversation in the front room had grown louder and more raucous. The effect of the drinking was audible. Jimmy continued to play for a while longer and then stopped. He did not move on his seat but simply hung his head over the piano keys. Mama's head had been lowered for some time.

Over the din of the talk, I had been listening to Yancey and I knew the moment the pianist stopped. For several minutes the noise of the conversation continued. Then someone realized there was no music.

"Play some more, Jimmy. Why did you stop?"

The voice rang out over the other voices. They all stopped talking then and called for more music. For a moment or two Jimmy and his wife remained motionless. Then Mama Yancey turned around on the bench. There was anger in her eyes. She had felt the humiliation of her husband. As she spoke, her voice was almost a shriek.

"Jimmy ain't no piano. He's a piano man."

All of those present, depending on their state of sobriety or drunkenness, were variously stung by those words. I was the least guilty of them all, and I felt the most pained. The Yanceys were artists, and now at the end of their lives they had to accept charity on Saturday nights from a few admirers who drank whiskey until they could no longer hear the music.

The scene was distorted for me, as distorted as my life had been with Seth and Judith. But I knew that whatever scenes there were still to live through that night, they would be the final scenes. I was suddenly happy in the distress of that scene at the Yancey's, happier than I had been for months.

Slowly at first, and then gathering momentum, the spirit of the drinkers came back into full force. They showed repentance under their banter and jokes. They apologized to Jimmy and Mama by mocking their hurt sensibilities. They charged the air with promises of love and kisses, until Jimmy, melting under the dulcet words and the slaps on his back, ran his sleek, nimble fingers over the keys and teased his visitors back into silence.

When a few couples again began dancing to Jimmy's music and the newly restored order had settled over the room, Seth made his way to the sofa where I was seated and settled down beside me.

"I'm drunk, or I'm almost drunk," he began, "but I know that something's going on in that head of yours. The lover of knowledge is thinking. And I don't like what he's thinking. I'm scared of it. Don't do anything for a while. Just promise me that. All will be all right. Why can't we be satisfied with this?"

Even before those words were spoken, I knew that Seth had invaded my thoughts. And I knew that Judith was aware of the interchange of thoughts. Our restlessness had infected her, and when her brother began declaiming, "I want a duskier place than this, I want to go to a duskier place," she sent me downstairs to get a cab and began preparing Seth for the trip home. He was by then quite drunk, but more dignified in his bearing and more haughty than when sober.

Outside it was a damp, drizzling December night. There was some snow in the rain. Seth, supported by Judith and me, raised his hand to feel the wet on his face. Again he declaimed, "Let that hooded phantom come now. Let me see that snow hill in the air."

Once he had slouched in the seat of the cab and stretched his legs, his mood changed to something lighter and to reminiscence. As he looked through the window, he detached himself from Judith and me.

"Am I the same guy who ran along these streets as a boy?" He paused then, and gave, not an answer, but a comment on his thoughts. "Life carries the body along. A man finally accomplishes his history, and yet there is nothing real about it, nothing more substantial about it than this snow that is falling flake by flake, and melting as it falls."

Seth broke into this with a rich, ringing laugh, and turned to me.

"Old man, he said, "our beards are stiff with icicles tonight! But do you know, I'm going to sleep with a harpooner, and in the morning one of us will leave for the sea, to find the hooded phantom of snow."

By the time the cab had reached the house, Seth had quieted down and had to be roused in order to get him out of the cab. I got out first and pulled, while Judith, from behind, pushed her brother. We supported him into the house and up the stairs. Not until the three of us were inside Seth's room did he straighten himself and push us aside. Judith and I watched carefully to see if he could stand alone. He smiled wanly as he held us off.

It was only a brief moment, and then Seth lost his balance and sank to the floor where he lay curled up with his head tucked down below his shoulders. That head was the basilisk under leaves, the piercing eyes concealed behind the lids, the feigned quiet and immobility, the waiting for the flash of life, for the return of life and the fatal glance of the eyes.

I straightened Seth out on the floor, turned the boy's head back with the closed eyes facing the ceiling. The paleness was there, as if all the blood had been drained off, and the hard shape of the face resembled a mask. Before I lifted him, I stood over Seth's body to gather my strength and smiled at Judith. I wanted to say to her there was no danger at that moment. No danger when the basilisk's eyes were closed. But Seth would soon again be hurt into consciousness. He would come back into life from contact with the floor and from exhaustion.

Judith set about undressing Seth. She took off his shoes and socks first, and then, helped by me, she propped him against a chair and took off his tie and shirt. I completed the undressing while Judith bathed her brother's face and hands with a wet cloth. Perhaps Seth was semiconscious of what was going on. He seemed to help a bit at the difficult moments when the full weight of his body would have made it almost impossible to put on his pajamas.

At last he was ready. I raised him in my arms, unsteadily at first, and carried him across the room to his bed. The tawny light of the lamp fell on the pillow.

Seth kept his eyes closed. He was breathing audibly. His presence had waned. His assertive bearing had diminished. There was even a trace of humility, of childlike humility on his face. I wondered if that very moment might be the bundling of a man into eternity. I had watched so many shifts of mood in Seth, so many efforts to seize some new hope or cast off some new resentment, that then in the peacefulness of that immobility I felt the end of a legend on me.

10. Haiti, January 1959

Between the two halves of the academic year, Bennington College traditionally closed its doors for three months: December 15 to March 15. "Nonresident term" or "winter period" it was called. For a French teacher like myself, it meant Paris—a chance to live in Paris without the hordes of summer tourists; to see the new plays, *le théâtre de l'absurde* of Beckett, Ionesco, and Adamov; to catch a few lectures at the Collège de France; to meet old friends at Les Deux Magots in Saint-Germain or at La Coupole in Montparnasse.

January 1959 was a different experience for me, although it was related to my continuing study of modern French poetry and to the translation of Saint-John Perse I had been doing. I had received a grant from the Huber Foundation to spend a month in Haiti where I was to interview Haitian poets and try to determine to what degree they had been influenced by French poetry.

After a few days in Port-au-Prince, where I lived in a small hotel on the Champs-de-Mars (reminiscent of Paris only in name), I began to realize that nothing takes place there as it does in the United States. All of life is played in a different tempo in Haiti. One has to learn how to submit to time and be acted upon by it. Especially, one has to learn how to wait.

Letters do not easily or quickly reach you. The solution is to write no letters. You send messages, but they arrive too late. And then you realize it was just as well, after all. At first, all practical matters seem impossible to accomplish. But then, mysteriously and unexpectedly, everything is accomplished, everything is ultimately carried out, and within the flexibility of another time. Very rarely do streets bear any visible name. And even more rarely do houses bear any number. People will describe to you in detail the site of a house and its façade, but they will be unable to give you the name of the street or the number of the house. Haitians carry in their minds the picture of a house, but not its address.

They will tell you fervently that you must see such and such a poet, but they will not tell you how to see him or where to find him. Then one fine morning, the door of your room will open and there he will stand. I have heard it said there are secret forces working for you in Haiti, and I can believe this. Mystery is everywhere in that country, but it is an active mystery, slowly efficacious. An American has to forget his country's utilitarian methods of communication, such as telephones and postal services, and learn to depend completely on the human, and on what is behind the human: the supernatural and the divine.

If everything seemed difficult to me from the visitor's viewpoint in 1959, it was infinitely more difficult from the Haitian viewpoint. The poverty and the overpopulation of the country, the economic life and the political life weighed as heavily on the poets as on the peasants. All of their lives are regulated by the same hostile forces. The Haitian people were born from an antislavery revolution, an overwhelming victory over the Napoleonic forces in 1804. The black population, over 99 percent illiterate at that time, was able miraculously, in a very few years, to create a literary elite. Poetry for some time remained an oral art. During the American occupation, in the 1920s, a group of young intellectuals formed around an important magazine, *La Revue Indigène*, and the figure of the novelist-ethnologist Jacques Roumain. Haitian poetry, as a recognized school, began at that time. With a combative aesthetics it concentrated on the Haitian patrimony and on a poetry in which the three cultures forming the Haitian school are fused: African, first and foremost, with its tribal customs, its cruelty and spiritual invincibility; European, with its aggressiveness but with its refinement and skepticism also; and finally, the Indian culture of the American continent.

During the late thirties and forties a few of these poets whose careers began with the pioneer work of *La Revue Indigène* published poetry which reflected the dynamics of Haitian history and which at the same time stood by itself as art, as a literary expression capable of holding its own with poetry being written in Europe and America. One poet in particular had been made famous by the attention accorded to him by André Breton, who visited Haiti in 1945. Clément Magloire-Saint-Aude is one of the authentic *poètes maudits*, surrealist by nature long before Breton called him surrealist. His name headed the list of poets I had read about and hoped to interview.

The second on my list was Jean Brierre, and he was the first poet I met in Port-au-Prince, during my first morning on the island. I was wandering through the business section of the city, along the rue des Miracles, not very far from my hotel. I was walking on the shady side of the street because the sun was hot that January day. On the sunny side I noticed a bookstore, *Librairie Indigène*, with the name "Jean F. Brierre, avocat." I wondered if the bookseller and the lawyer could also be the poet. I crossed the street into the sun and into the store, and there I recognized the poet Jean Brierre from the photograph I had seen in Selden Rodman's book on Haiti. He seemed a man of thirty, and yet I knew he was close to fifty.

With his first publications in the early 1930s, Jean Brierre had been acclaimed the national poet. He had sung of the history and the vocation of Haiti as few poets had. He had been schoolteacher, school inspector, and diplomat. He had studied at Columbia University and had lived in Paris and in Buenos Aires. I had found his most recent poems, "La Source" and "La Nuit," both published in Lausanne, more abstract, more "cosmic" than the earlier patriotic works. I was to discover very soon that he was still an eminent figure in Haiti, a national bard, but that his reading public was not the same as it had been in the thirties and forties.

Jean Brierre's bookstore was a meeting place and a center for the poets. I soon realized that if I returned often enough, I would meet all the poets. Brierre's kindness and generosity to me were limitless. In a quiet, unobtrusive way, he brought about a desired meeting, related a message, proposed a visit. He waited on customers (in this he was admirably helped by his wife Dilia), greeted the many friends who stopped by each day for a few minutes or for a long conversation, attended to some of his legal work, and kept beside him a notebook in which new lines of poems were inscribed during the intervals between his many activities.

My visits with Jean Brierre in his bookstore, which served so many purposes, gave me my first insight into the coherent, unified world of Port-au-Prince. Haiti is a large family. The writers form one branch of this family. When together, they speak with the intimacy and naturalness of members of the same family. They attended the same schools, watched the same religious rites in the forests and villages, participated in the same Mardi Gras processions, and now teach the children of their former schoolmates.

My first morning in Port-au-Prince, in Jean Brierre's *librairie*, I bought what I could find of Magloire-Saint-Aude: the poem called "Déchu," the prose poem "Veillées," and the story "Parias" (which the poet called a *documentaire*). There had been three others (all of them thin pamphlets); "Dialogues de mes lampes," "Tabou," and "Ombres et Reflets." I had told Brierre that morning that I was aware of the importance accorded to Magloire-Saint-Aude by André Breton, and I had read the warm testimonial written by William Jay Smith in 1952. Even that first morning I sensed in Brierre and in others who stopped by the bookshop a hesitation to tell me anything specific about Magloire. They tried to change the subject after saying that he was difficult to find, that he was an alcoholic, not well in health, who lived in a willed solitude.

This kind of answer was to be repeated many times to me throughout my month in Haiti, and made me more eager than ever to meet the mysterious poet. His revolt against society was already legend, confirmed by his few published works. From the beginning I was being helped in every way in meeting other poets and tracking down their publications. At first, I felt certain that I would come upon the most illustrious of them all, but by the end of my visit I had serious doubts that I would ever meet him.

On my first Sunday morning in Haiti, Jean Brierre invited me to a gathering of poets at his home, for the express purpose of discussing poetry and reading poems. I was curious to learn which of the French poets were read and admired by the Haitian poets. Rimbaud was often referred to as the permanent "classic" of those younger men. They also expressed a predilection for Saint-John Perse, for Apollinaire, Supervielle, Eluard, and Aragon. And yet the poems I heard recited that morning owed little or nothing to the poets of France. I asked for a Creole poem of Morrisseau-Leroy, "Diacoute." (The word means a peasant's bag.) I knew this to be a dramatic poem, and it was entrusted to the outstanding actor of the group, Clovis Bonhomme, who was playing Creon in the Creole version of *Antigone*. M. Bonhomme, who was director of the Collège Sainte Marie, had a rich, harsh voice. He read, like one inspired, those poems about the impoverished life of the peasants. Regnor Bernard read his poem "Altitude," a song of praise of the black race. René Bélance read a new unpublished poem, "Geôle," on the suffering and the fatalism of the blacks. Jean Brierre read a passage from the long poems he was writing at the time, "Sillages," and then, as homage to the absent poet, Emile Roumer, read Roumer's much anthologized "Prends garde." All those poets read with the finesse and intensity of professional actors.

My presence in Haiti had served as the immediate reason for that Sunday morning gathering, but the poets decided, at the end of the morning, to continue such meetings. The political and economic problems besetting Haiti had become alarming, and such gatherings had been given up or postponed. That morning the poets acknowledged the need to resume the custom of reading and listening and discussing in the presence of one another. I marveled that morning at their capacity to transcend the pressing problems of daily existence which all of them were feeling.

As they spoke or recited, they seemed to recapture something of their inner life, the grace and seriousness of their dreams, the pathos of their spirit. There is something of what the French call *dolorisme* in the Haitian character. There are traces in their behavior and in the expressions on their faces of the mute eloquence of the slave trying to liberate himself from his suffering. I heard the tragic and noble history of Haiti in the voices of those poets as well as in their poems.

My encounters with the writers were varied. Each was different from all the others. And yet certain characteristics of temperament and feeling kept reappearing. After all, the family traits of their small republic were in evidence everywhere. They spoke, for example, always with respect for the secrets of the *vaudou* rites, and yet they all seemed to live by the conviction that there are more secrets in the heart of a man than in the ceremonies of *vaudou*. These men all had a common ideal built on a belief in the perpetual progress and evolution of mankind. Their poems were written from the cries, the emotions, and the anxieties that are common to all their people. Men who had visited the island and met some of the poets—Aimé Césaire, for example, André Breton, and the philosopher Jean-Paul Sartre—quickly realized that those Haitian poets had a lucidity of intellect that penetrated the realm of dreams and opposed it to conscious reality. In some of their most moving poems, they recall surrealist practices.

The sincerity of these writers has sometimes been called naïveté by critics who see in it only a lack of reticence and reserve. It is far more than that. It is a need these writers all feel to live, even instinctively, the heroism and the idealism of the national heroes. But the past of those heroes is more than historical. It antedates recorded history. Such age is in the poets, such age has formed them, that today when they speak of writing poetry, of "singing," they say they will always "sing," because that is equivalent to living.

When I lived in Haiti, in 1959, there was no literary magazine and no publishing house. But there were many poets, some of whom were worthy of being published and whose works would have interested readers in other countries. The Haitian poets know one another and form a clan, with older and younger members. Largely, I suspect, because of this intimacy, there has never been any criticism of poetry. From approximately the end of the American occupation of Haiti in the early thirties, the poets have written with the determination to forge a new poetic language, purely Haitian. Prior to that time, the art of poetry on the island had been a literary exercise, a servile imitation of the French poets, both in theme and form. Sully Prudhomme, Leconte de Lisle, Heredia, and other Parnassians from France were the models. The national consciousness of Haiti, an awareness of the country's own individuality, of its own problems and aspirations and way of life, became the contemporary themes sung by the poets. A new poetic language developed with the new country. At the time of my visit, when Haiti was living through an economic-political crisis of the gravest kind, the poets were somewhat silenced by the suffering and anxiety they were sharing with their compatriots.

It was already difficult for me to find the small pamphlets of poems published between 1940 and 1959. Those *plaquettes*, published at the expense of the poets themselves, were badly printed, on poor paper, and they had become rare items for collectors. Occasional poems appeared in the newspapers, but I was confident that the newest and youngest poets were unpublished and unknown. Those poets who then taught in the *lycées* and *collèges* encouraged their most gifted pupils as once they had been encouraged by their teachers.

The poets in Haiti are known as poets and are respected as such, despite the variety of professions they represent. As Jean Brierre was a lawyer and ran a bookstore, Félix Morrisseau-Leroy was director of a small theatrical company (*Théâtre d'Haïti*) and *metteur-en-scène* of his own plays and of others. René Bélance and Regnor Bernard were teachers of Haitian literature at two or three of the *lycées*. Magloire-Saint-Aude worked for the newspaper *Le Nouvelliste*. Roussan Camille was also a journalist. He had recently interviewed Fidel Castro in Cuba. The novelist Jacques Alexis, whose two novels had been published by Gallimard in Paris, was a physician and neurologist. Milo Rigaud had published an important book on *vaudou* and was preparing a treatise on the *vévers*, the emblems or designs traced on the ground with flour during the *vaudou* rites.

Those men were serious about their writing. They had no desire to imitate the French or be looked upon as French writers. In my conversations with them, they often referred to the visits of André Breton in 1945, and of Jean-Paul Sartre in 1946, because both the poet and the philosopher had encouraged them to continue the kind of writing they had initiated: an indigenous creative writing, purely Haitian, based on the traditions of the land itself, on the folklore and religious practices, on the persistent problems of the black race as they had been manifested in the past and the present of Haitian history.

Haiti is a land of two languages: French, the official language, spoken by the educated, used in the schools and on all formal occasions; and Creole, that curious amalgamation of many languages, but basically French, which is spoken by everyone and is the only language of the large peasant class. The poets were still debating on the advisability of adopting Creole as the official language of poetry. Emile Roumer, one of the older poets, a resident of the town of Jérémie, had rejected French and was writing exclusively in Creole. During my first week Port-au-Prince, I came across a series of sonnets by him, written in Creole and published in the *Haiti Sun*. One of those sonnets was on the seventeenth century French poet Saint-Aman, and another on Governor Faubus of Arkansas!

I was unable to visit Roumer in Jérémie, which is some distance from Port-au-Prince, but on the day before my departure I received a poem from him in Creole (six stanzas of twelve lines each) in place of a letter. It was in reality a manifesto in favor of Creole as the better language for the Haitian poets. French he called a language poor in accents, which has to count its syllables and needs rhymes. It is, in short, an antipoetic language, "a beast with a thousand feet."

> Francé, pauvre en accents, pour obvier maladie
> besoin rimes ai oun compte syllabes pour extropier;
> langue anti-poétique, cé oun bête à mille pieds!

Roumer announced in that letter-poem that he was translating *Othello* into Creole. A younger Haitian poet, whom I had seen on several occasions, F. Morrisseau-Leroy, had made an adaptation of *Antigone* in Creole and had produced it in a new theater company which he had founded in Port-au-Prince, and which had then moved to Pétionville, just south of Port-au-Prince. The success of that play had been so marked that Morrisseau's company was invited to Paris to perform at the Théâtre des Nations (in May 1959). He claimed it would be the first play in Creole ever to be performed in Paris.

Creole is softer and more fluid than French, an easy-flowing, rhythmic language which seems to have as many cries and sounds as actual words. I was assured many times that the richest expressions in Creole are untranslatable into French. One of the still unsolved problems for the poets is the lack of any authoritative system of spelling in Creole. Roumer's spelling, for example, is different from that of Morrisseau-Leroy. And there is the equally unsolved problem for most of the poets in Haiti of which language to use. It is difficult, perhaps unwise, for a poet to write in two languages.

Two meetings were especially meaningful in both a literary and human sense. One took place on my last evening in Haiti. My plane for New York was scheduled for an early-morning departure. I had not succeeded in finding Magloire-Saint-Aude, and had given up hope of reaching him after countless efforts and inquiries.

I was eating dinner in my hotel's dining room, alone at my usual table. The dessert had just been placed before me. Suddenly I realized someone was quietly standing beside my table. I looked up and saw a tall fellow whom I did not recognize. Without smiling he said to me: "Tu cherches Magloire-Saint-Aude?" I replied in French: "Yes, I have been trying to reach him for a month. No one has been able to help me find him, and this is my last night in Haiti."

Laconically he said: "Suis-moi." I left my untouched dessert and followed the mysterious figure out of the hotel. I had already learned that chance often comes unexpectedly in Haiti. My guide was a businessman (*homme d'affaires*, he said), not a poet, who had heard of my futile search. "I will take you," he said, "to the small house where Magloire now lives alone, in an almost total kind of isolation."

The section of the city was called Martissant. Before we reached the house in the center of a wooded area, I heard the loud blasting of a radio playing jazz. My guide left me then. "Just walk in—you'll find him there." I felt nervous, ill at ease, as I pushed the door and entered a brightly lit room. A somewhat large man was seated before a table in the center of the room directly under a bare electric bulb hanging from the ceiling. His back was to me. As I came up to him, I could see over his shoulder the book he was reading: *Vents* by Saint-John Perse, the large edition open and spread out on the table.

I remember saying to myself that *Vents* would make a fine introduction if there was any difficulty in starting a conversation. The radio music was so loud that I had to touch his shoulder. I introduced myself and asked if I might ask him some questions about his work and French poetry. His greeting was shy but cordial. Not until we began speaking of poetry did he relax. As I asked my first bungling questions, he showed signs of distrust. With good reason.

I could not explain why I was so deeply moved at seeing him. It was, first, his actual physical resemblance to Rimbaud, to the few photographs of Rimbaud in the last years of his life in Africa, where his skin was tanned by the sun, when he was dressed in loose-hanging clothes, unshaven, grown old before his time. Magloire-Saint-Aude was not yet fifty, but he seemed older. There were a few streaks of white in his hair. When he laughed, everything about him became youthful, even his face which was heavily lined and his eyes which flashed from behind thick glasses.

Moreover, the life he led at that time was similar to Rimbaud's in Africa: the simplicity of his house and his withdrawal from all social life. Rimbaud, of course, had lived far from home during his last years, whereas Magloire was living in his native Port-au-Prince, where he had spent all his life save for a few trips to other towns in Haiti, notably Cap-Haïtien and Jacmal. The literary resemblance between the two men had struck me as I had read the few pages of Magloire-Saint-Aude I had been able to find. The elliptical strong prose of "Veillées" and "Parias" had reminded me of "Les Illuminations." The poet of Port-au-Prince combines a metaphorical originality with a direct and often cruel observation of the world, a combination which is one of the traits of the Charleville poet.

The final trait of resemblance was the Haitian poet's indifference to his own work. He told me he had given up writing poetry, and spoke of his early work objectively as if he were no longer responsible for it. He seemed eager to speak of poetry, but not of his own, eager to discuss the French poets but not himself. When at one moment in the conversation I mentioned Saint-John Perse, he turned and pointed to the *Oeuvre Complète*, volume one, on the table behind him. He said he had been reading *Vents* throughout the day, and was amazed and delighted to learn that Perse was born in his part of the world, on a small island off Guadeloupe. "Un poète authentique, celui-là," he said half to himself and half to me.

Clément Magloire-Saint-Aude spoke with admiration of Breton's visit to Haiti in 1945. He was well aware of the fact that Breton had granted him a place among the surrealists, but he repeated several times that his work had been written before he knew much about surrealism.

In "Veillées," the last of his works to be published, in 1956, he reveals the talent of *romancier maudit*. The story is reminiscent of Poe in its macabre quality, and of Rimbaud in its clear, strong sentences. The poet is attending the wake of a young girl, Thérèse, who did not die in a normal way. During the course of the evening the poet becomes aware of life in the corpse. On this last page of the work, the closeness which the Haitian feels to the supernatural is admirably transcribed:

> On avait placé des cierges au chevet de la trépassée. Soudain, la flamme d'une des bougies vacille, à reprises, comme sous l'haleine d'une présence occulte, et s'éteignit.
>
> Les autres lumignons, comme à un signal, l'imitèrent.
>
> Dans le demi-jour qui suivit, Thérèse ouvrit grands ses yeux, des yeux étrangement beaux, d'une gaieté sensuelle, inconvenante jusqu'à la cruauté.

Je me fis violence, et je parvins à me lever, comme un automate, pour clore les paupières de la défunte. . . . L'épouvante glaça mon sang et une légère fumée s'échappa de ma veste.

Mais une sérénité indicible, tout-à-coup, inonda mon coeur, pendant que je portais le tuyau de ma pipe à mes lèvres.

Tous les invités étaient partis.

Depuis une demi-heure, l'angélus avait tinté au clocher de la cathédrale.

A l'orient, les étoiles pâlissaient.

They had placed candles beside the head of the dead girl. Suddenly, the flame of one of the candles lowered several times, as under the breath of an occult presence, and went out.

The other lights, as at a signal, imitated it.

In the half-daylight which followed, Thérèse opened her eyes wide, eyes strangely beautiful, of a sensual gaiety, unbecoming, even cruel.

I made an effort and succeeded in rising, like an automaton, in order to close the eyelids of the dead girl. . . . Fear froze my blood, and a light whiff of smoke came from my coat.

But suddenly an unspeakable serenity swept over my heart, as I raised the stem of my pipe to my lips.

All the guests had left.

Half an hour ago the angelus had rung in the cathedral steeple.

In the east the stars grew pale.

The world evoked by Magloire-Saint-Aude in his writing is that of drunkards and pimps and young *voyous*. He caught the intonation of their tragic voices and the sense of dereliction in their lives. He respected his characters and their enigmas, and made no attempt to explain them or excuse them. They too had their understanding of the inexorable continuity of life.

We talked for two hours in that small house in the forest of Martissant. At the end, at my request, he read, or rather recited from memory, this poem from "Veillées" about the dead girl Thérèse. My last question was a burning one, and I almost did not ask it. I phrased it awkwardly in this way: "Why have the other poets whom I have seen and talked with discouraged me from trying to find you?"

"I will tell you," he said. "The reason is very simple. They probably said I was an alcoholic, and that is true. I am. However, that is beside the point. They have turned against me for political reasons. Our president, Papa Doc, is aware that I am the only Haitian poet who is known outside of Haiti. In that sense, he is proud of me and gives me a monthly subsidy which keeps me in rum and pays a woman to bring me one meal a day and clean this house. So, you see I am being supported by the man whom they believe is bringing ruin to the country."

As I left Magloire's house and walked back to the hotel, I remembered Carlos Saint-Louis as being the most adamant of the poets in urging me not to see Magloire. Saint-Louis was a poet by virtue of the very tension of his entire being which he lived with every day. It was a tension without artifice, a state in which his soul appeared proud and exalted. Haitian poetry is composed of all the cries and spasms of man, as well as those noble passions current in the poetry of every age.

The major accents in the writing of Carlos Saint-Louis are decidedly of the Negro race, and obsessively sad. It is the poet's lucidity bent upon understanding dreams and contrasting them with the so-called experiences of reality. The opening of "Aux plus beaux d'un bel avenir" is a striking example of the Haitian poet's will to oppose the sordid aspects of daily existence that offer no hope.

> Aux plus beaux d'un bel avenir
> je reprendrai de beaux accords
> Le monde aura couleur d'amour
> et l'abandon couleur d'oubli
>
> Me rencontrer tel que moi-même
> et me recontempler vainqueur
> convertir les espoirs déçus
> et renaître à la source vive
> dira pour les jours de malheur
> une aube vierge où chanterai
>
> From the most beautiful ones of a beautiful future
> I shall take back beautiful harmonies
> The world will have the color of love
> and desertion the color of oblivion
>
> To meet myself such as I am
> and contemplate myself again as conqueror
> to convert deceived hopes
> and be reborn at the live source

> a virgin dawn where I shall sing
> will speak for the days of wrath.

The Negro soul believes in a future which he constantly sees in an hallucination. He needs to recall the glory and the power of national heroes. His culture today continues to be nourished on the spiritual remains of a glorious and tragic past.

Two nights prior to my last evening in Haiti, when I met Magloire-Saint-Aude, I had another unexpected encounter which today, as I look back on the entire month in Port-au-Prince, seems to me the most exhilarating, the most deeply moving encounter of my entire visit. I knew the name of Jacques-Stéphen Alexis, but since I knew him to be essentially a novelist, I had not made a specific effort to meet him.

He was in Port-au-Prince —I had been told that a few times—and was a practicing physician attached to the hospital. In my desire to meet many of the poets, and in the pressure of time which was running out, his name had dropped from my list. Moreover, I was limited to daytime visits and almost always stayed in my hotel after dinner. I had been warned several times not to walk alone after dark in the streets of Port-au-Prince. The times were ominous, and there were frequent murders, carried out by the guards or the soldiers or the spies of Duvalier.

I had finished dinner and retired to my room on the second floor. A firm, clear knock on my door surprised me because it was the first visitor who had come in the evening. I opened the door and there in the semidarkness of the hallway stood a tall, thin, very dark-skinned Haitian, more handsome than most of the Haitian men, very much at ease in his relaxed posture, with a smile on his face and an expression of curiosity about seeing me, obviously, for the first time.

"Jacques-Stéphen Alexis. Vous ne m'avez pas encore cherché. Je suis donc venu vous voir moi-même."

It was the French of a Frenchman, although the timbre of the voice was Haitian. He used *vous* instead of *tu*. There was, above all, a directness, a total naturalness in his manner that I had not yet experienced in Port-au-Prince. In my first words I tried to match his manner.

"Est-ce que vous arrivez de Paris plutôt que de votre hôpital, cher docteur?"

He laughed and came into the room. We talked at first, not about Haiti but about Paris, where he had studied at the Ecole de Médicine and had spent those years of study in happiness, excitement, even rapture, he said, at living in such a place, in an atmosphere of freedom.

That word *liberté*, as I think now of Jacques Alexis, was the leitmotif of our conversation. It turned out to be a long evening visit, divided into acts almost, when the freedom of his life in Paris as a medical student was constantly being contrasted with his threatened life as a boy and later as a doctor in Haiti. Of all the writers I met in Port-au-Prince, Jacques (we used first names almost immediately that memorable evening, as if it would have been scandalous to do otherwise, and soon used *tu* rather than *vous*) spoke the most directly, the most unguardedly, about the political situation under Duvalier and the sense of danger he lived with each day.

When I made certain that he had planned to spend some time with me that evening, I suggested that we walk to a bar where I could offer him a drink. The small hotel bar was open only before dinner. He declined and said, in an almost matter-of-fact way, that his name was on a list of condemned men, that it would be unwise for me to be seen with him in public.

"My old Ford car is outside. Let me drive you to a few spots you have not seen, backcountry roads that will be visible when the moon rises tonight. There is less danger for me and for you too if we stay in the car and keep driving. I am proud of the Haitian countryside, and I want you to see it. It is almost your last night, isn't it?"

Before we left my room, Jacques asked to see what Haitian books and pamphlets I had found and to check the names of the poets I had interviewed. "Here is one of my books to add to your collection," he said, as he handed me a large volume with the familiar Gallimard cover on it: *Les Arbes Musiciens*. "It is the most recent of all you have, since it was published in Paris in 1957. I wrote it partly in my town of Gonaives where I was born, and partly in Port-au-Prince, where I am classified by the secret police as a suspected communist. I waited until almost your last night in Haiti before coming to see you in order not to throw any suspicion on you. The poets you have met have not been outspoken as I have been against the Duvalier tyranny. . . . Now let us go into the night and into my Ford. We can talk as we ride and no one can hear us."

I had heard a few eminent French writers speak to me in Paris about their work and their career, but no one had been more eloquent, more movingly articulate than Alexis that night in Haiti. He spoke of his love of writing with the enthusiasm of a very young writer. He was thirty-eight years old, but looked twenty-five. Throughout the evening I marveled at the freshness, the exuberance of his spirit. And yet I knew him to be of the race of sufferers.

In that year of 1959, some of the leading citizens of Haiti were living in the *maquis*—the dark of the island forests—those men whose lives had been threatened more directly than the life of Alexis. He knew the secret passwords and kept in touch with these men as closely as possible. Since he was a physician, especially competent in neurology, his life was more useful to the government. But he was under constant surveillance.

I asked him if he wrote because of the troubled times. He replied that was only one of the reasons. He wrote first very young because of his love of French, of its incisiveness and of its powers to express his imagination, the images that are fixed in his mind and that need words to communicate them. But ever since finishing *Les Arbres Musiciens*, the very explosiveness of the concept of freedom had held him.

"You will find all my themes in *Les Arbres Musiciens*: the life of the peasants of my country and the urban proletariat, the esoteric rites of *vaudou*, the history of Haiti, and my love for Haiti."

We stopped from time to time on the back roads where there was a view Jacques wanted me to look at: a farmhouse beside a pond, a clump of mango trees, a rise in the land now lighted by the moon. There he would apologize for sounding like a patriot. I told him that his patriotism sounded to me like that of Émile Zola and Anatole France. He smiled then and put his arm on my shoulder.

"Yes," he would say then, "love of my country and love of justice are in me, but also a daily fear of death and its inevitability. The poets express that in their poems, and I try to avoid it in my books. They find my attitude toward the Catholic Church negative, resentful. But they are wrong. I love the Church when it fights for justice. The poet I used to see most often in Paris was Louis Aragon, and we talked of the Church's role in the future."

Paris and Port-au-Prince, France and Haiti, were often joined in our rambling conversation, as we drove over country roads, and returned circuitously to my hotel on the Champs-de-Mars. That evening was my longest single visit with a Haitian writer. It was the most dramatic of all my visits, and the one that most clearly articulated one man's life in its dreams and realities.

Three days later I took the plane for New York, and there above the clouds began to read *Les Arbres Musiciens*. I found it to be a novel as impassioned as I had found the speech of Jacques Alexis to be on that improvised moonlit night.

Two years later, in 1961, I learned that Jacques Alexis, returning to Haiti from a trip to Cuba, had been captured by the secret police and stoned to death.

11. Nice—La Trappa, 1975

After Paris, I know Nice best. Paris for me is the excitement of literature and history, the beauty of squares and boulevards, of churches and museums, of gardens and bookstores. Nice has another kind of beauty, where I enjoy the effect of the sun on the sea and the villas, where I watch the combination of nature with the works of the Niçois in their hotels, in their Promenade des Anglais, in their dark castle at the summit of the promontory, and in all the smaller sites close by: Villefranche, Eze, Vence, Cassis, La Napoule, Saint-Jean-Cap-Ferrat. Paris for me represents the past of France—in its memories of writers, in the actual houses where they lived and died, in the streets where they walked, and in the cafés where they drank their aperitifs as they argued politics and literary theories.

I have had seven or eight visits to Nice, of a month or two each time, in the same hotel, in fact in the same room of the same hotel, number 428—a room with a view of the distant Alps. No great writer was born in Nice. When I come to the Atlantic Hotel, I give up my fanatical search for the sites of writers—their houses and streets and restaurants—and have to be content with collecting phrases extolling Nice, written by writers who have lived there at various times from the eighteenth century on, and who have enjoyed living there as I have. I join their ranks gratefully as I measure the kind of pleasure I have felt with the pleasure to which they have given a literary expression.

Most of the passages extolling Nice that I come upon are from French writers. But I am well aware of the cosmopolitan character of the city, where country houses on the outskirts and villas inside the city are inhabited by English, Germans, and Russians, as well as by French. This state of affairs has been going on for more than a century, since colonies of foreigners began settling there for the sun and the sea, for retirement in a slow-moving, sensual life. Nice is a serene place, and I have always felt serenity in me when I have lived there in my Atlantic Hotel. I welcome such serenity, foreign to my nature, in that Mediterranean setting so totally exotic for a Yankee.

Each day, and often twice a day, I walk to the sea, which I find smooth and calm. Yet if I walk in the direction of *la vieille cité*, I find it foaming on the rocks. I breathe the air—so warm and fragrant—into my lungs. It always smells of orange trees. Along the road to Villefranche I come upon heather and broom. Purple and yellow seem to be the colors of Nice. The old part of the city is my favorite walk, where all is brown and yellow. Patches of shadow cast by the houses alternate with lively patches of sunlight.

What splendid parks Nice has! They stand out in the poorest and richest neighborhoods. The very young children own these parks where they play in the sandpiles, and the very old men own the benches where they sit hours on end and watch the children and sometimes talk with them. I have enjoyed listening to that dialogue of the very young and the very old. It is usually a philosophical dialogue of questions and ideas, carried on under the shade of trees until youth tires of age, and age nods its head under the barrage of excited questions shrilly asked. The questions will not be answered. This is the ancient world of the Mediterranean where the warmth of the sun turns questions and answers into what they really are: a game of the spirit renewable each day.

I leave the park I have visited in late morning and pass the hedges covered with ivy and myrtle. I walk then in the direction opposite to the Alps and make for the sea, "the bay of angels," *la baie des anges*. May has always been the best month, when I can hear at the same time the song of the frogs and the murmur of the sea. On those late morning walks, when I need an escape from work in room 428, Nice was mountains, rocks, flowers, and sun on its acropolis-like castle. Attic bees are buzzing in golden broom (*genêt*). Purple anemones are blooming, and irises with their amethyst petals. It is spring after Easter, but I have several times known spring in December or January in Les Alpes Maritimes.

The Niçois: a populace of actors engaged in a perpetual comedy. They seem happy, these inhabitants of Nice. They molest no one. They eat well and drink in moderation. The visitors and the writers walk on the Promenade des Anglais, but the Niçois stay in their stores and restaurants. They might walk briefly around the old harbor and on the Place de L'Ile-de-Beauté, or on spots from which they can see the Estérel, the mountain on the horizon, a mauve arabesque.

Nietzsche was here once, in the Hôtel Continental on the rue Verdi, and enjoyed the mildness of an ideal climate. D. H. Lawrence died in a small villa in Vence, high above Nice in the *arrière-pays*. Chagall once lived in Vence before coming to Saint-Paul-de-Vence, where he died in the spring of 1985. I lived briefly at the Fondation Camargo in Cassis, closer to Marseilles than to Nice, and there I often thought of Katherine Mansfield who lived in Cassis about 1920. Eze, on the top of a hill on *la route de la Corniche*, was admired by George Sand. Once I took the bus from Nice to Grenoble, which closely followed *la route Napoléon*.

It is a landscape of dreams, a land of contrasts where everything exists for the pleasure of the eyes: sun, blue sky, crystal horizon, multicolored land, dazzling gardens, a perfect sea with its curved *rivage*, and a spacious city welcoming those visitors like myself from every country.

La Trappa

The invitation came at just the right time during my three-week vacation in Nice. It was my eighth visit, and I had begun to fear that nothing unusual was going to happen. My tendency has always been to repeat the routine of living, to rediscover the familiar rather than to discover the unexplored. I believed I knew all the pleasures of Nice, at least all of those in my hotel on the boulevard Victor Hugo.

The telephone call from Saint-Paul came early in the day, about 8:30, when I was settled into some writing after finishing off, with my usual greediness, the café au lait and croissants. Even my morning greediness never varied. Two friends, one French and one American, invited me to join them at dinner in a restaurant in the old section of Nice they had just discovered and thought I would like to know. My "yes" to their invitation was spontaneous and delighted. They would pick me up about six at the hotel, and we would go on foot from there. On the telephone, Alain and Rowland were evasive about the name and the exact site of the restaurant. This was predictable because the restaurant was to be a surprise. Through the day I enjoyed savoring the unknown and made no effort to learn what the name or location might be.

I was in the lobby at six, engaged in conversation with my English friend Mr. Knight, a resident of the hotel for over twenty years. When my friends came in, I made the introductions and we spoke briefly of Saint-Paul-de-

Vence, where Alain owned a small house and where Mr. Knight had once lived with his wife at La Colombe d'Or. Then the three of us left Mr. Knight for his traditional dinner in the hotel dining room and set out on foot as planned.

In order to break the walk, we stopped for an aperitif at the café close to that point of the city where "le vieux Nice" begins. Our talk moved easily into matters at home in North Carolina. Rowland and Alain lived in Chapel Hill, and I lived in Durham, eight miles away. We spoke of big and small changes: of the growing power of President Ford and of what seemed to be his non-liberal moves, of the plans for the new hospital at Duke. Then we spoke of changes at hand: the new management of the hotel La Résidence in Saint-Paul, and, from my viewpoint, the lack of changes in the Atlantic. My friends had often chided me for endlessly returning to the same old spot. I had stopped long ago trying to defend my case of the traveler who repeats his travels and experiences of the year before, and even of the years before.

On resuming our walk we passed by the large government building on the rue de la Préfecture. It is a fairly long street I knew well and remembered that it terminated in the very heart of old Nice. "We will be there when we reach the end of the street," Alain announced quietly. After a few more minutes I could see the façade of the restaurant I had often passed on previous walks and had wondered about. La Trappa was the name, in large, pointed letters.

"Yes, that is where we are going," Rowland said, almost begrudgingly, as if this precise knowledge of the restaurant would diminish its mystery. I assured my good friends that all would be new to me inside those doors, that indeed this evening was to be a new experience.

It was not a restaurant for tourists, except for such tourists as we were, familiar with Nice and lovers of the city. La Trappa: the Italian form of the word related the past of the city to the present, and I was already imagining— what in reality I was to find inside—a half-Italian, half-French restaurant. It was early for a Nice restaurant when we entered—about seven-thirty. The waiters were clearing off the center table where they had been eating.

The handsome, long wooden table, extending from one end of the room to the other, turned La Trappa into a kind of *pension de famille* where diners who wanted to talk with others would sit, and where an atmosphere of conviviality would be induced. On either side there were small tables. The general effect was that of a nave lined with side altars. A large bar, on the right of the entrance door, could easily be the high altar. The numerous bottles of various shapes on shelves behind the bar caught the light from the overhead lamps and provided the effect of candles in this ecclesiastical image.

One of the waiters gave us a choice of side tables, and we took one near the door from which we would have a full view of the restaurant, from the bar down the full length of the center table to the door leading into the kitchen. My eyes first caught a large basket of fish placed on the center table just opposite our own table. The fish glistened too, like the bottles over the bar, under the overhead light. At the far end of the long table, and facing our side of the restaurant, a lonely figure of a young man sat and studied the menu. He was not a Latin type, but probably a tourist like ourselves, American or German perhaps.

By this time the waiter was back at our table with a menu for each of us. His resemblance to the actor Alain Delon, in his earliest films, was striking. When I mentioned this fact, he smiled and said, "You are not the first to tell me. I'd like to see one of the films of that fellow some day and watch myself." He seemed pleased at the recognition, and, since we were the among the first customers, hovered about our table as we began to consult the menu.

It was handwritten and very clear. Opposite each of the items, arranged in three groups, was the same price of six francs. I had never seen that uniformity on any menu. The very first dish in the hors d'oeuvre group attracted all three of us: *pâte au pistou, six francs*. This would be an Italian beginning for three hungry diners. *Pistou*, with its flavor of basil, I had known especially in a Provençal soup, and I was curious to taste it in a noodle dish.

In the menu's second group I noticed the elliptical form: *loup, six francs*. This was of course *loup de mer*, which I had never eaten but which I knew to be the most celebrated fish from the Mediterranean. The translation? I am not sure even of dictionary translations, but it may be "sea bass." When I asked the waiter for *un loup de mer*, he turned to the basket of fish on the table behind him, picked up one and asked if it was big enough! A *loup de mer* from a fresh catch already seemed a new treat from La Trappa. Young Alain Delon assured me it took only two or three minutes to cook over the blazing kitchen fire. My two friends ordered *une dorade*, the Mediterranean fish I usually had in any typical Nice restaurant.

Then I began reading the meat dishes in the third category. The last one of the five or six listed was the surprise: *testicules, six francs*. I had never before seen this particular organ on a menu. The waiter was smiling as I read it out loud, as if he were waiting to see the effect on me. So I asked him, "Les vôtres?"

"Non!" he replied, "testicules d'un mouton."

At that moment the single client at the center table must have been puzzling over the same item. His finger was on the menu and he was trying to ask his waiter, in a confusion of languages, whether the word was a joke or whether it was really what he thought it was. The waiter was answering him in a few loudly articulated monosyllables, including, "ici, ici," and therewith grabbed his crotch. It was an explicit language lesson with gestures.

The tone of levity changed to seriousness then at our table, when our waiter explained that La Trappa had two "spécialités de la maison": *testicules* and, for dessert, *tarte à l'orange*. That item, too, I had never seen on a menu and never tasted. I decided that for me the *pâte*, the *loup*, and the *tarte* would be sufficient, and that I would omit the *testicules*. But Alain did order the *spécialité*, and later gave me a sample bite or two, enough to satisfy my curiosity and not enough to bring on any possible squeamishness.

By the time our three orders were given, the restaurant was beginning to fill up, and when we left, more than two hours later, every table was taken. Unable to be seated, the latecomers were by then standing three deep at the bar, and the linguistically paralyzed young man at the center table was indistinguishable, if indeed he was still there.

The very light green *pâte au pistou* was delicious and quickly relieved the pangs of hunger I had been feeling for the previous hour or two. The *loup de mer* was the best-tasting fish I had ever had. I had known of its reputation, and learned at La Trappa that the reputation was fully deserved. The small mouthful of *testicules* reminded me of the taste of sweetbreads. The *tarte à l'orange* had a slightly burnt taste that offset its sweetness and made it into a perfect denouement of a surprisingly novel and thoroughly delectable dinner. Whenever he passed our table, whether he was bringing food or not, our Alain Delon waiter delighted us with his amiability and wit. But we realized he was a *charmeur* for every table and provided the entertainment before the appointed entertainer arrived.

This man was a dwarf, a singer accompanying himself on a guitar, who suddenly appeared in the aisle by our table. His voice was rich and strong and easily dominated the noisy conversation in the restaurant. He began his performance when the three of us were waiting for our *tarte à l'orange*. So we heard him for about thirty minutes before leaving La Trappa. When he passed us, his head was level with the top of our table. The fine quality and strength of his voice were in keeping with his handsome face and the breadth of his shoulders. He moved slightly back and forth in the aisle beside our table. From that spot he easily projected his voice through the entire room, and he succeeded from his first song in attracting attention and approval from diners at all the tables, and from those clients behind him, standing at the bar.

So the vigorous singing of the dwarf was new for us as we ate, for the first time, the *tarte à l'orange*. The waiter, who had recommended the *tarte* as a *spécialité*, asked our opinion of it. We were complimentary as we were informed that the recipe was a secret carefully guarded by the restaurant.

La Trappa was the needed interval, the novelty that added a new dimension to my Nice of May 1975. As Rowland and Alain left me at the entrance to the Atlantic, and I entered the hotel lobby quite deserted by then, I marveled at the chain of events initiated by the unexpected early telephone call from Saint-Paul-de-Vence that morning. The day-long expectancy of the evening had given me a greater willingness to carry out the familiar habits and routines of the day. By the next day the restaurant had become a series of scenes giving me the effect of a collage: the bewildered client questioning the menu and his waiter's obvious gesture of explanation; the light green color of the *pâte au pistou*; the exhibition of the *loup de mer* destined for my plate; the learning about edible testicles and the small portion at the end of my fork; the orange pie with its crust burnt over an open fire; the vigorous singing of the dwarf guitarist. Yes, the memory of the menu and the events of La Trappa lasted through all the remaining days at Nice . . . and thereafter.

Whereas *la trappe* in French means both a Trappist monastery and a "trap," such as the "trap floor" into which Ubu hurled his opponents, *La Trappa* in Italian seems to have only the religious meaning: *un convento di trappisti*.

12. Villa Serbelloni, 1981

I arrived Sunday, July 12, 1981, in this spectacular place, after a long, tedious night and day in planes and airports. On Saturday Rowland Fullilove drove me to Raleigh-Durham airport. There I took a plane to Kennedy, and waited for four hours to get on the 747. Then we waited an hour in the plane before departure. Seven hours later we reached Malpensa Airport in Milan. After a long wait for my bags to emerge, there were a few anxious minutes before I saw a man, presumably from the Villa Serbelloni. It was Gian-Carlo, an expert driver who had worked fifteen years for the Villa.

Between Malpensa and Serbelloni there were ninety kilometers to cover, of which the last thirty (Como to Bellagio) are difficult: a steep, narrow, winding road along the lake. Magnificent scenery all the way, but a dangerous road (at least to me). My apprehension was not relaxed even when Gian-Carlo told me the road has been in continuous use since the beginning of recorded time.

We finally drove up to the Villa Serbelloni, an almost legendary property for two centuries, red-roofed, ochre-walled, with formal terraced gardens sloping to the lake. At the entrance door the housekeeper, Signora Ardovino, and two *camerieri* stood waiting for me. Each *cameriere* took one of my bags and Mrs. Ardovino led me to my room (number three) on the ground floor. A long, spacious, beautiful room with a balcony—my gym, I was to call it, for exercising—looking over *il lago di Como* on one side, and *il lago di Lecco* on the other.

Bellagio is a promontory that has figured in Italian history since the Celts came in 500 B.C. The Romans came in the first century. Pliny the Younger in his letters speaks of his Como villa and of this cliff overlooking the lake. In the thirteenth century the area was the battleground of the conflict between Guelfs and Ghibellines. The castle of Bellagio (*il castello*) passed from the Visconti family to the Sforza family in the fifteenth century when it became a fortified city. At the end of the eighteenth century the promontory passed by bequest to Alessandro Serbelloni, of a great Milanese family.

In *La Chartreuse de Parme*, Stendhal records his impressions of the villa. After the last Serbelloni sold the villa in the mid-1800s, it served as a luxury hotel for sixty years. Ella Holbrook Walker, of Detroit, when she became *principessa della Torre e Tasso*, adopted it as her home and renovated the villa. In 1959 she offered the villa, plus two million dollars, to Dean Rusk, then president of the Rockefeller Foundation, to be used as an international conference center.

All of that history was in my mind as I enjoyed the first full day in the villa. The day of my arrival I must have seemed tired to Mrs. Ardovino. She suggested that I have lunch in my room. A tray came at one o'clock, and then I tried to rest. Too tired to rest! I joined the group of "scholars" for drinks and dinner. John and Pam Blum from Yale greeted me—we were friends of Catherine Coffin. Pam was writing on Saint Denis and we talked of the basilica. I read until ten (a most comfortable bed) and then slept soundly until six. I felt more like myself in the morning and did a bit of writing. I knew I would do more as the novelty wore off.

I was constantly reminded of two other places I have lived in. First, of Yaddo, because of the routine and the use the villa is put to: a group of writers (and one composer) working separately and meeting at meals. They were excellent meals, beautifully served by two or three *camerieri*. I was also reminded of the San Domenico Hotel in Taormina because of the magnificent site—especially from my balcony—and of the language I tried to speak with the *cameriere* and *camerieri*. Also similar were the elegance of the villa itself and the many comforts that were given me there: an Olivetti typewriter, mineral water and crackers in my room, a bell to ring for a maid if I needed one, and another bell to call a steward if I needed him. A thermos of *caffè e latte* was left in my room after dinner, for my early rising. (Breakfast is not served until eight.) Aperitifs were served before lunch and dinner, coffee and liqueurs after lunch and dinner.

On my second day members (twenty-seven in all) of a conference on food and world famine had begun their work. French seemed to be the official language. I walked down the 299 steps carved out of steep rock leading to the town of Bellagio and easily found an excellent barber and a bank. The climb back up the stairs was hard on me, and I imagined I would not go down to the town more than once or twice a week. After the Blums, I talked with Dr. John Bowers who is writing the history of the foundation's health program, and who turned out to be a friend of Bill Anlyan at Duke. The small group of "resident scholars," seven or eight, who worked here for a month, was quite distinct from the conference members who stayed five days. Each week there was a different conference.

Thanks to the thermos of coffee left in my room the night before, I could begin some of my memoir-writing between six and eight o'clock. After breakfast I worked on Baudelaire's aesthetic theories, trying to fill out the chapter on Baudelaire and Delacroix. After lunch I tried to write a bit about the Villa Serbelloni, and a bit in the chapter on Chicago I planned to call "The Basilisk." A full schedule, typical of so many others I have been engaged in for fifty years!

After a few days I was accustomed to the villa itself, to the food, so delicious and abundant, to the view of the lakes and the mountains, and to the feeling that I was really in a sanatorium where I was working in order to save my life and survive. In a sanatorium or on a boat, cut off from the world. The others around me, as we talked before and during and after the meals, kept making plans for excursions to get away for a few hours from the fortress. I welcomed the idea of living in a fortress or a sanatorium where all the practical problems are taken care of.

On other visits to France and Italy, I always found it tiresome and even disagreeable to wait in line in a post office and have letters weighed and then stamped appropriately. Not here at the Villa Serbelloni. I wrote a letter, sealed it in an envelope of the villa, addressed it, and in the place where the stamp would go wrote my name and dropped it in a box outside the dining room. A secretary the next morning picked up that letter, weighed it in her office, affixed the correct stamp and inscribed the amount under my name, so that at the end of my four weeks I was presented with a bill for my postage.

Everything was done to liberate one for work and for relaxation. I mentioned to Franco, the head steward, that I needed a laxative. That evening when I returned to my room a *cameriere* had left on my table a bottle of *Olio di Ricino*, with a spoon and directions to take three spoonfuls before going to bed. The next morning a large bottle of prune juice was left in my room. (I realized it behooved me to be healthy in this villa.)

James Vorenberg, one of the seven "scholars", was dean of the Harvard Law School. He had just begun his new tenure before leaving Cambridge with his wife Betty for the Villa Serbelloni. The first day or two he had seemed a bit distant and even haughty, but then feelings warmed up between us when he discovered I had attended Brookline schools. It turned out that his father, ten years younger than I, attended my two schools: Edward Devotion School and Brookline High School. One evening after dinner he led me down the stairs through the garden to a small, circular chapel where he worked during the day. He was tall, almost athletic in his walk, a very self-possessed man who appeared to have reached a high point in his career. He knew Ken Pye (our chancellor at Duke) and thought highly of him. Both men studied criminal law. In that fortress isolation, strands of the past and possibly of the future were soon joined. I was firmly held in the present moment by all I had lived through in the past.

A curious social phenomenon took place between the small group of scholars and the large groups in the conferences. All was friendliness and courtesy when we met at the table for meals, but they knew and I knew that there was no time to establish any bonds, and we somehow forced the conversation to remain on a superficial level. Ironically, a few of the conference guests appeared to me more interesting to know than some of the more permanent scholars. From Friday lunch to Monday dinner, the six of us, with four wives, were alone, thrown together for every meal. The most friendly to me, in a quiet way, was Bob Cox from York University, and the most enigmatic was Jim Vorenberg from Harvard Law.

As the first week drew to a close, the pattern of existence at the Villa Serbelloni grew clear. The hours went by too slowly. I missed the routine of running my own apartment and cooking my own meals. Sleep was deep and sound in my comfortable bed under heavy blankets. It must have been like death because I moved back into the past in dreams recalling many figures I once knew. I saw what once had occurred around me, and had no fear of it. During the day, when I was alone so much of the time, I thought often of death and the peace it will bring me. Death is the destroyer of all images and stories, and I suppose that is why we will do almost anything rather than face it. Can one love in the great ranks of the dead? That question kept returning to my mind all one day. (I mean love of other human beings.)

The thought of death was for me the same as the immediate future. I sensed it as a vibrating darkness. I was close to it, closer than I had ever been before. By comparison with me, at my present age, this Villa Serbelloni was the symbol of eternity, a shrine really for the *principessa della Torre e Tasso*. Death will happen one day, as love happened one day in the past. All human life is compacted of accident and composed of chance. Gate after gate in my mind seemed quietly to open. The past was all about me in that place where I was a stranger.

After the hours spent at the dining room table three times a day, and the thirty minutes drinking coffee after lunch and dinner, I escaped to my room with a feeling of sadness for the human race. We are such natural prattlers. The scholars in the villa and the conference members kept on talking, as I did, and I wanted to shout to them that our hearts are too corrupt to know truth. The multiplicity and the randomness of their speech appalled me, as I am sure my speech appalled them.

Perhaps in this Villa Serbelloni I learned to do something about the past. It just does not cease to be. It goes on existing and affecting the present. Let me take up again the perennial task of examining my thoughts and my instincts. Are we condemned to some endless, incomprehensible search?

I missed the young in this place invaded by the middle-aged or those a bit younger. They were either excessively pleasant and uttered the same polite remarks about the villa, or they tried to engage you with the heavy jargon of their profession. Yes, I missed the young because the young do not really know how wretched and vulnerable every human heart really is. I realized there, more acutely than in most places, that the training society gives us deprives us of the finest language of the heart and the direct language of love.

Too much polite conversation—and that is all the Villa Serbelloni allowed —depresses me, and I gratefully took to the shaded walks that stretched out in every direction on this promontory. But that exercise tended to turn me toward my own thoughts, as my writing periods did. If I were walking in a city street, that would be different. I picked up a few books from the library shelf and enjoyed them: *La mort d'une mère* of Roger Peyrefitte and *The Road Through the Wall* by Shirley Jackson.

The Peyrefitte book, soberly and admirably told—about the actual death and burial of his mother—brought back to me my own mother's death, which occurred at a time when I was traveling by plane between Denver and Boston. I contrasted in my mind the piety of Peyrefitte's mother and my own mother's piety, so similar in a fundamental sense and so different in all exterior aspects: a Catholic mother dying alone in a convent, and a Baptist mother dying alone in a nursing home to which the doctor had sent her the day before her death, when she had entered a coma. The Catholic mother's son was devoted and a nonbeliever. The Baptist mother's son was devoted and a Catholic! The two funerals were equally unreal and embarrassing for both sons.

The Shirley Jackson book, about Californian suburban life, presents a large group of children, well-drawn, mysterious, and tragic, and a large number of adults who seem more stereotyped. As I read her book, I could almost hear her voice and remembered the few good talks she and I had on the piazza of her North Bennington house. She was a gifted woman and as mysterious as those children she shows us in this novel, children doomed by their background, their parents, their playmates, and their early unacknowledged sexual drives.

On my second Sunday in Bellagio (July 26), as on the previous Sunday, I went down the 299 steps to the village (called *un paese*) to attend mass in the attractive Romanesque church of San Giacomo (with its fine *campanile*). I reached the church early, about 9:20, planning to go inside to rest from the long descent to the lakefront, then explore the town and return for the eleven o'clock mass. I had been seated just a few minutes in the back of the church when a priest in vestments entered from the sacristy and took his place at one of the side altars. It was obvious he was going to celebrate mass alone, and I moved over to a seat close by him. He gave no visible sign that he knew I was following his mass, until he came to the moment just before consecrating the Host. He turned then directly to me, and, holding the Host in his hand, asked "Il corpo di Cristo?"

"Sì, padre," I answered, "vorrei condividere con Lei." A few minutes later he gave me half of the consecrated wafer. Was I the *principe* of the Villa Serbelloni, having my mass said in private?

Each morning I left my room at five minutes to eight in order to arrive at the dining room at eight for the earliest breakfast possible. I went through the long hall, where at various points there were large clusters of flowers beautifully arranged in vases. Two in particular I noticed: two kinds of daisies, one yellow and red, the other a pure yellow. Each morning at exactly the same time I met an old gardener checking the flowers and sometimes replacing them. He was Carlo. We always greeted one another. One morning I asked him the names of the two kinds of daisies. He knew the names but at that moment could not remember them. He was embarrassed, and I was too. I wished I hadn't asked him. But the following morning we met in front of the same vase and he told me the two names—long Latin names they were. A good man, Carlo, and proud of his work.

Two more books replaced the two earlier ones, one in French and one in English, which I enjoyed reading in late afternoon and early evening. I had seen the films based on these books, but I had never read them: *Papillon* by Henri Charrière, and *To Kill a Mockingbird* by Harper Lee. The law is in both books: the murderer Charrière, condemned to life imprisonment, and the working of the law in a small Alabama town in 1935. *Papillon* is a long

chronicle—an autobiography—of a man escaping from prison, being recap-
tured, escaping again, in a series of South American seaport towns and prisons.
I enjoyed the language and the courage of Papillon, and his honesty, far greater
than that of his judges and jailers. I read pages out loud each day and inscribed
idiomatic phrases from the language of French prisoners in my practice-
language notebook.

The title of the second book is taken from the phrase: *It's a sin to kill a
mockingbird*. A mockingbird does no harm. It sings for us all day. In the story the
mockingbird is a black man falsely accused of raping a white girl. The story is
told by a very young girl, Scout. The affection she feels for her brother Jem, a
few years older, and for her father Atticus, a lawyer, is skillfully narrated. The
book avoids sentimentality and gives a strong analysis of sentiment and honor.

A few hours of reading rounded out my day of writing on three projects, of
walking on the promontory, and of three meals usually followed by conversation with other residents. I told myself it was good for me to be away those
four weeks, but each day I longed to be home. Almost each day someone left,
and I caught myself saying, "Patience, my time will come and I too will leave
this elegant fortress." I feared that such elegance, such comfort, such continuous attentiveness were not conducive to real work.

Each morning I watched the dawn glimmer over the surface of the two
lakes seen from my balcony—Lecco and Como—and I liked that part of the
day best, when all was quiet, the guests were sleeping, and the forty people
who worked in the villa and on the grounds had not yet come.

I enjoyed talking with Roberto Celli, the director, and with his wife who
read Rimbaud and Proust. At table I often sat with Robert and Jessie Cox who
were Canadians. He taught political science at York University. I asked Robert
to give my greetings to Hédi Boursaoui, a faithful friend of many years since
the summer we met at Bennington. There was a couple from Chapel Hill
(John and Dale Reed) and a couple from Ann Arbor (Jean and Jake Jacobson).
At the end of my stay I met Jackson Cope, a friend of Bruce Wardropper,
from the University of Southern California. Jackson was there with his young
wife Paula.

I grew impatient to be home, with the tiresome plane trips behind me and
the welcome resumption of familiar routines. What would I find in my accu-
mulated mail of a month? Who would telephone me first?

13. Room 520, Loyola Hall, College of the Holy Cross, 1982–83

The two elevators in Loyola Hall are efficient and swift. In less than a minute I reach the fifth floor and walk down the long corridor. The rooms on each side are numbered and bear on the door in large letters the name of the priest who lives there: Fr. ———, S.J.. My room, 520, is normally reserved as a guest room for a visiting Jesuit, but during the school year my name was on the door, preceded by *Prof*—the only layman in a community of sixty-four Jesuits.

In late August when I arrived in Worcester, Massachusetts, to teach for a year at Holy Cross, I sensed, but only faintly, that a few of the older priests (three were in their eighties) were puzzled by my presence among them and behaved shyly if we met in an elevator or sat at the same table in the dining room. By the end of the first month—to myself I called it my period of "postulancy"—I had encountered on all sides, from almost every priest I met at meals, at drinks before dinner, or in the TV room in the basement after dinner, signs of cordiality and acceptance.

Loyola Hall is no Trappist monastery (that is ten miles away in Spencer, and is often referred to—approvingly—as a place for retreats, and as a leading example of the traditional cloistered monastery) but rather a well-run hotel-pension for the Jesuits who lead active, useful, and varied lives. Only a small percentage are teachers. (Two are French teachers like myself—Father Alfred

Desautels and Father Lionel Honoré—and lived on my floor.) Others are administrators or work in hospitals or serve as confessors for Worcester citizens.

Each one has his own personality, and his own way of thinking about the Society of Jesus, politics, the pope, the Israelis in Beirut, the celibacy of priests. Soon I felt I knew character traits and idiosyncrasies in several of those with whom I spoke most often. Before I engage in general thoughts about these men, I want to write out a few details of behavior in some I observed.

At first, Father Vincent Lapomarda seemed gruff, almost curt in his greetings. A large man with a protruding belly, he walked fast, usually carrying more than one newspaper under his arm. When I arrived in the fall he mentioned he was forty-eight years old, a teacher of American history, and about to go to Europe and the Holy Land for a few months. He is one of the very few Holy Cross fathers with an Italian name, but he does not speak Italian.

Every evening, between 6:30 and 7:30, I joined a few of the priests who regularly watched the TV news in a basement room set aside for that purpose. Vincent often came in a bit late and sat down in the third seat of the first row while I sat in the first seat on the left. He used a footrest which allowed him to stretch out. His apparent indolence was purely physical, because mentally he was very much alive, fully concentrated on the news and commenting on the pictures and what was being said. If he came in when the commercials were on, he usually turned to me and said, "Wallace, what is the news so far? Anything important?" When the commentator spoke, the room was silent save for Vincent's explosions: horror at scenes of horror, cries of approval at justice being done, disgust over what deserved his disapproval. Vincent enlivened the show for me. I missed his presence during the weeks he was away, and I missed the clippings from several newspapers he slipped into my mailbox, such as a map of Assisi (we had once spoken of Assisi at lunch), an article on Taizé in Burgundy, obituary notices: John Gardner, Alexander Coffin, Tennessee Williams, Rebecca West. At first I had wondered where these came from, and soon discovered that Vincent registered what interests I had expressed in conversations and cut out from the many newspapers he scanned articles he thought I should see. Of course, he also did this for his brother Jesuits.

By his speech, his thoughts, his activities, Vincent was the most ardent of the Jesuits there—a seemingly contented man. He was writing a book on the Jesuit holocaust. When I learned at the beginning of the year that he was on sabbatical leave, I asked him if he missed teaching. "Not in the least," he replied, with such vehemence that I thought my question must have sounded stupid to him.

A few of the Jesuits lived in dormitories and came to Loyola only for meals.

I was interested to see what type of priest, what type of man, preferred to sleep in a dormitory, on one of the boys' corridors, not as an R.A. (resident advisor) but presumably as a quieting presence of an older man. One was the new dean, Father Raymond Schroth. This was his second year at Holy Cross. A year earlier it was he who had hired me. When he was editor of *Commonweal* we had corresponded about review assignments he gave me. I had looked forward to meeting him in person. I found him a tall man, thin and vigorous, a runner (five to eight miles a day), with a gaunt face, flashing black eyes, easy of speech, withholding of his closest thoughts. Across his face, as I spoke with him, flashed two alternating kinds of expression: approval and suspicion.

Ray was a man in authority, exercising his authority by almost daily notices of various kinds sent through campus mail to faculty and students. I agreed with him when he urged students to read more, to become more unashamedly intellectual, but the directness of such urgings made some (students and teachers) indignant. He was alone, perhaps the most isolated of all members of the community. He wanted to serve, but the manifestations of his ardor were awkward. He played squash, swam, ran, lived in Mulledy (a student dormitory), held long conferences with individual students, but gave (falsely, I think) the impression of coldness, of aloofness. Inwardly he was not cold, not aloof. What a fight was being waged in that man's heart!

One Sunday night in March, he sat down for supper at the table where I had already begun eating with four other Jesuits. In total innocence, I asked if Gerard Manley Hopkins had ever been a candidate for canonization. Ray said no, and pointed out that biographers of Cardinal Newman and Father Hopkins had hinted at traces of homosexuality in the temperament and even in the writings of both men. All of us at the table concurred in believing this was not enough reason to deny canonization if in other ways these men qualified.

Father Earl Markey, who lived in Lahey dormitory, gave a similar impression of strength and power. He was tall too, heavyset, with white hair, an open face, tanned. He did not smile, but he laughed when there was something to laugh about. He served as dean of students. A former basketball player (according to the legend), he appeared at times gruff, which was only part of the macho image he projected. I imagined he was a disciplinarian who loved those he disciplines. He might have become a coach, but he became a priest whom I may see celebrate mass some Sunday at eleven, the mass I usually attend, and I expect then to see him transformed into God's servant.

The youngest and handsomest Jesuit was Father Michael Boughton, still in his thirties, a recent arrival (two years earlier), and an assistant chaplain. Large, strong-looking, but probably not strong, he worked directly with a large number of students in conferences and retreats. He lived with them in Wheeler dormitory, and was admired, I imagine, by the girls, and looked upon by the boys as a man who might have been a coach and a close friend. He was a fervent celebrant at mass, and a fervent homilist.

The same priests tended to use the same tables in the large dining room at breakfast, lunch, and dinner. (It was the same situation at Kimball where I took three dinners a week with students.) The same groups of students ate together at the same tables, near or far from the salad bar. In both dining rooms I strove to be the first to sit down at the table which I had selected as my preference, in order not to impose myself on priests or students. I was the visitor, unknown as a friend, recognized as a French teacher from Duke, really an intruder. I spoke with 120 students three mornings a week in the classroom, and with two or three students during three dinners a week at Kimball—and seldom at any other time. I spoke with a small group of Jesuits three times a day at meals—and never at any other time save for the most casual of exchanges in the elevator, or in the TV room, or for thirty minutes before dinner if I joined them for drinks in the lounge adjacent to the dining room.

Thus an exchange of words between me and someone else took place frequently between 7 A.M. and 7:30 P.M. The teaching hours were the best, when I strove to make myself useful to those students who had elected to read some literary texts with me. All other exchanges tended to be brief and therefore casual, on the point always of being ended. The tone, with students and Jesuits alike, was always friendly and cordial, but I didn't see how it could have gone beyond that. Life was busy and active for everyone. The priests had mass to say and other priestly duties to perform (these were not visible to me), and the students had sports, study, meals, TV programs, bull sessions in their rooms, and parties. I am trying to say that my life at Holy Cross was filled each day with many encounters, with study and personal work, with class preparations, with nine classes each week, but it was at the same time devoid of any meaningful relationships with students, Jesuits, or lay teachers who far outnumbered the priests.

In other words, my life during 1982–83 was quite similar to every other year, save for this absence of a few close friends and several good friends. This absence of human relationships was of course due to the lack of an apartment of my own. I was pampered at Loyola, where I lived in a hotel-like situation: a large comfortable room impeccably cleaned each week by two housekeepers. meals served downstairs, a TV room, my own post office box on the first floor. I was asked not to receive visitors in my room. A few small parlors on the first floor were reserved for that. So, room 520, despite its attractiveness, was for me alone, living like a celibate in a monastic cell. Such solitude and quiet are admirable, and I often enjoy them in my North Carolina apartment, but there I'm able to break them with short and long visits from friends. I want celibacy and I also want to be able to break the rule (and the situation) of celibacy. Yet this experience of 1982–83 was one that I had wanted to know.

Toward the end of the first semester a few of the priests began saying to me, "When are you going to join up? It is not too late to come into the Society. There is a center you can attend for 'late vocations.' "

At first I took this to be a mere pleasantry, but it continued into the second semester and I realized it was serious. Once, Father Desautels, my best friend there and my colleague in French, said to me: "This year will count as your first year." One day in November, Father Pomeroy, who was driving me to Pittsfield, said, "For all intents and purposes you are a Jesuit *donné*." The term was used in Canada and this country in the nineteenth century to designate a man who lived in a Jesuit community but who was not a priest and had taken no vows. He led as closely as he could the life of a Jesuit without being one. There have been *donnés* martyrs.

When I asked what they did, I learned what I already half-suspected, that they performed hard manual labor: cutting down trees, building chapels and houses. I replied, with a slight degree of relief, that I was not up to that, *à mon âge*. He showed no hesitation in tossing back the words: "The three courses you are giving this semester will count as three oak trees felled."

Finally I hit upon a rejoinder that to some degree quieted down the almost daily urging to consider changing my way of life. At lunch one day, when four priests were present at my table and one began rehearsing the now familiar theme, I said in a serious tone of voice, "I am waiting to be named a cardinal, because a cardinal does not necessarily have to be a priest." They had forgotten that law, and I, too often the tiresome pedant, reminded them of Mazarin at the court of Louis XIV, cardinal but not a priest, and, in more recent years, of Paul VI's desire to make Jacques Maritain a cardinal, and the aging philosopher's request that he not be thus honored.

Of all the obstacles to such a change of vocation at my advanced age, the one I cannot imagine ever overcoming is that of being called "Father." Such a title would be the result of ordination to the priesthood, and such a title, used a hundred times a day for each priest at Holy Cross, would signify a responsibility for which I have not been created and which I have never wanted. "Father" is for God only! I would not want anyone, not my own child, if I had one, to call me "Father."

With all the changes taking place in the Catholic Church, one that I would advocate which I have not yet heard advocated is the abolition of the title, "Father," and the substitution in its place of the more humble term, "Reverend." In a few instances a student has called me *maître*, or addressed me that way in a letter. That word too horrifies me, because instinctively throughout my life I have tried to prove to students and friends, to those younger than myself and older, that I am a helper and not a leader. When a student whom I have known well "graduates" with a B.A. or a Ph.D., and thus moves into the better and more simple category of friend, I suggest he use, as a sign of such a transition, my first name or my baptismal name "Michel." Such a transition was smoothly accomplished when I was thirty. It is harder in these later years. Age is a terrifying psychological as well as visual barrier.

Here in room 520 where I spent so many hours alone, so many long stretches of afternoons and evenings, I caught myself seeking out groups of memories to see if out of them I might form a history. The days, the meals, and the companions at those meals became so predictable that I forced myself into an unusual inner life. Because of the closed-off solitude in 520 (I knew this and agreed to the situation before I entered Loyola Hall), I was less able this year to live in a constantly renewed and refreshed moment of time. There was little skill left in me in improvising my moments and making each one distinct from the other. All improvisation had gone into my dreams, richer, more lurid, and more striking than my usual dreams these last years. When weary of the sheer solitude of these hours at Loyola, I retired early with the thought that dreams would take over and fill my mind with unpredictable actions, with characters I half recognize, with scenes taken from off-moments in my life that merge together to create a new scene.

Thanks to dreams, then, I continued to be peopled, even in my solitude of room 520. At each decade I have found some device, depending on where I am living, by which I can foil or exploit the particular solitude in which I find myself.

In my teens, in order to escape my Brookline solitude, I explored Boston on foot, or rather I repeated favorite walks beginning at the Public Garden, continuing on Beacon Street up past the State House, Louisberg Square, Dartmouth Street, the Boston Public Library, and all of that general area, including Trinity Church, S.S. Pierce, the Copley Plaza. Without exactly living there, I appropriated as my own site those parts of Boston. I was a Bostonian then, proud of the city's history, of its European-like beauty, of its distinctiveness — the "hub" of the universe! By comparison, Brookline was pale and dull. A suburb: a marginal place I grew instinctively to deprecate. Cambridge was far better, because of Harvard's prestige and M.I.T.'s. From early childhood I planned to study at Harvard and knew that I would find Cambridge more compatible than my native town.

Thus in my late teens and early twenties, I lived in a world where scholarly solitude was necessary for survival, where it was welcomed, in fact, as a time allowing an inner growth of knowledge and a new awareness of the past. As I read French literature, first, and then studied philology during my graduate years, Cambridge became the site of a gigantic library, of classrooms inhabited by students, many of whom seemed hostile or aloof, and with whom I had to compare myself in knowledge and style and speech. That was the solitude during which I prepared for my vocation, to which I joined the solitude of prayer and meditation in the chapel of the Cowley Fathers on Charles River.

In the next period of my life I knew the solitude of the teacher, necessary for the preparation of classes and the correcting of papers. This merged, almost every day, with the solitude necessary for my attempts to write about French poets and novelists, and it has lasted until today when I have recently completed my year in room 520 in Worcester, not too far from Brookline and Cambridge and Boston. This was a solitude unique in its own way because it was *almost* the solitude of a monastery.

I have to say "almost" because the Jesuits are not monastic, not contemplative, not solitary men. They do not recite together the hours in their chapel. They do not keep silence during meals. Their meals, which I enjoyed during this year, are brief periods of time, for eating and light talk: politics, sports, news about the pope and parish churches and Jesuit high schools.

Whenever Father George Barry was at my table, the conversation often centered on etymologies and moot philological problems. George is one of the most learned linguists at Loyola. (And there are several.) He always had an answer for whatever word I asked about, although he often added with a smile that it was problematic. "Serendipity" we spoke of once, and I have not yet learned a good use of the word. "To saunter" was another. Might it possibly come from *sainte terre* and the pilgrims headed for the Holy Land? "Pumpernickel" is a hard one and might come from Napoleon and the name of his horse, Nicole. When he was once told there was no white French bread for his breakfast and was shown dark German bread, he said, "That is *pain pour Nicole.*" The explanation of a boy being the "spit and image of his father" was a revelation to me, when George reasoned that "spit" referred to the sperm ejaculation.

Was I a displaced person during my year in room 520? To some extent, yes. It was inevitable. I felt, but never too steadily, never too strongly, the uneasiness of not belonging. The Jesuits often joked about their actions and their words as being "too Jesuitical," but they might easily resent someone outside the order using the word in the familiar derogatory sense.

In my French course, when we came to Pascal, I made a point of telling my students that I had never before attempted to teach Pascal in a Jesuit institution. When the class began understanding something about Jansenism and Pascal's attack on the Jesuits, one girl raised her hand and asked, "Dr. Fowlie, aren't you a little more Jansenist than Jesuit?" My answer was simply, "Yes, I probably am." "Well, I am too" was the unexpected reply.

I told the story that night at dinner, and I remember Father Lapomarda's sternness when he exclaimed: "Did she really say that?"

14. Lexington, Virginia, 1983–84

During the five years following my retirement (1978–84) I moved about considerably to teach for a semester or for a year in colleges that needed a "visiting professor": the University of the South (Sewanee, Tennessee); Duke University, as an emeritus; Holy Cross in Worcester, Massachusetts, for one semester and then on a return visit for a year; Virginia Military Institute in the fall of 1983; and Washington and Lee University in the winter and spring terms of 1984.

These last two, located side by side in Lexington, Virginia, proved to be not rival institutions, as I imagined them before coming to Lexington, but peaceful neighbors, each observing the other with considerable curiosity. I was told that in earlier years, when they have opposed one another on the football field, there had been vociferous hostility, filled with expletives of the strongest brand expressed Saturday afternoons each fall.

The town of Lexington is small, attractive, and proud of housing the two institutions, one of which is state-run and the other independent. As I moved about during the first weeks there, in late August and early September, introducing myself as a visitor the first semester at VMI and the second semester at Washington and Lee, the same reaction was always repeated: you will see two very different schools, two different types of students. The industry of the town seemed to be education: the high school and the two colleges. Everyone who was not working in a store seemed to be working in some capacity in one of the three schools, or had worked there and was now retired.

I was housed "on the post" at VMI, at 303 Letcher Avenue, a large old house made over into two apartments. My part of the house was well-furnished, comfortable, spacious—far more space than I needed, with three bedrooms, two living rooms, two television sets. I was midway between my classroom in Scott-Shipp Hall and the town post office where I received my mail. It was a six-minute walk in each direction. On my way to Scott-Shipp I passed the parade ground and had full view, as I approached, of the barracks, the spectacular central building of VMI, housing 1,300 cadets. Battlemented parapets. The fourth floor, occupied by the freshmen, always referred to as "rats," was the first to light up at six o'clock each morning. One of the many servile duties of the rats is to wake up the seniors (or first-class men) living on the first floor.

These were some of the new terms I tried to learn as fast as possible: "post," "rats," "barracks," "first-year cadets," "honor court." It was a scene, active and impressive, unlike any I had ever lived in. Yet my life remained essentially the same: early morning stint of work, some exercise, my walk three mornings a week to my classroom 216 in Scott-Shipp to read Dante with fifty cadets: twenty-five seniors, twenty-four juniors, and one sophomore. That walk to school at seven A.M., an hour before my two classes, never failed to stimulate me. I would see in a distance, in front of the barracks, companies of cadets forming to march to breakfast in Crozet Hall. There was time then to pick up mail in my department office box, to settle into my classroom and review my notes of the day for the two classes at eight and nine. Almost every morning one or two cadets would drop in for questions on the lesson, if they had been on guard duty at the time of the previous class. Class attendance was obligatory. The cadets formed outside the building and marched to the classroom.

During the classroom discussion and the review sessions in my house I held the evening before a test, the attitude and behavior of the cadets differed slightly from the comportment of students in other schools where I had taught. They asked questions more easily, with greater frankness, and they asked questions related to the cantos but not specifically about the text itself. There was very little time for social visiting. In fact, most cadets did not have enough time for studying and sleeping. The rule of "lights out at one A.M." was not always observed.

I had constantly before me, because of the closeness of my house to the parade ground and the barracks, a picture of the society of young men—the healthiest-looking men I had ever taught—moving out from the chaos of sleep into an ordered day of classes and exercise, of study and guard duty and parades. In such an atmosphere, when a sense of chaos filled me too, I explained it as coming from two causes of importance to me that were in peril: my own survival at VMI and the survival of what I was teaching. The use of literature had always been for me to breed in us a feeling for the passions and the needs of mankind. Nothing less than that! The best moments in a classroom can give a feeling of plenitude and sharing. At VMI I wondered about the proper conditions to develop the military man and the scholar. The *Inferno* is stocked with great military figures. The cadets seemed to pay more attention to Farinata and the battle of Montaperti, and to Guido da Montefeltro and strife-ridden Romagna, than to Pope Nicholas III in his pocket of stone, or even to Francesca in her windstorm.

As rocks hide fossils, so those fellows hide strength and passions and thoughts under their uniforms. Life in the barracks is predictable for them. I tried in the classroom to make it unpredictable to some degree. VMI is run in such a way that the cadets have to live in a state of constant alert, of constant obedience to an officer or to a rule. The political and military agitations throughout the world—the killing of U.S. Marines in Lebanon, for example—affect them directly. Students in other colleges live more precariously—they know more lapses and breaches in their years of study.

When I was asked to suggest a course to teach at VMI, I did not realize how suitable Dante would be. It would be the study of a great poet's art, but Dante would not coincide exactly with the modern concept of the artist seeking freedom of mind and immunity from practical affairs. Dante had been a prior of Florence and then exiled from his city for twenty years. The other type of artist—Giotto, Keats, Mozart—was more familiar to the cadets: the man alienated from the active citizen's life. Art, after all, was the first luxury to be discarded in times of stress. Yes, my students knew that society is the artist's paymaster and his patron.

In canto after canto as I prepared them for these new classes, I had to attempt to make clear the concept that pleasure is part pain. But I had encountered this problem in other classes elsewhere: the evidence of two emotions incongruously coupled in a man, which torment each other.

As time wasted fast for me in my house on Letcher Avenue, time moved slowly for the cadets who greeted me courteously as I walked to and from Scott-Shipp Hall and as my cadets reading Dante took their places in classroom 216. Their military life of constant exertion and exercise was too strenuous for any prolonged periods of study (unless they broke the rule of "bed by one A.M."). If there were any free moments after such a regimen, the cadets engaged in a remorseless analysis of falling in love and falling out of love. An all-male institution exerts great pressures on every member to have a girlfriend at home or in Lexington or in one of the many nearby women's colleges of Virginia.

I imagined that many such girlfriends were "made up," fantasized, to keep in the spirit of the place. In many ways the American concept of love, for college students at least, is close to the concept of courtly love as it grew in the second half of the twelfth century, in the big courts of the *midi*, such as Toulouse, and in the court of Marie, *comtesse de Champagne*, in Troyes. There she patronized Chrétien de Troyes as he elaborated the theory in romance after romance. From the twelfth century comes the obligation to love, to be in love, to name the girl, to write to her, to telephone her, to have her appear at the major festive occasions, the "ring" ceremony, in particular, when the junior (second-year man) is given a ring—his alliance with VMI. For which he has paid dearly in sweat and in dollars.

I say "obligation," because that is term from *l'amour courtois*. A well-bred chevalier could not escape it; neither can the cadet at VMI, despite his bustling life when he has little time to dream of love. It is an accepted fact that he believes in it, whether the girl be fantasy or real. The all-male world in which he is plunged, from reveille to taps, demands that he speak of love and show a picture or two of his love. The more infatuated he claims to be, the more relieved he will be from possible taunts leveled at him from roommates and classmates, yes, even from teachers and family. These cadets are only partially mature males. Just a step backward, when the uniform suddenly seems strange to them, they have the boyish gait, the lightness of heart of a sixteen year old, the laughter of a youngster performing some devilish trick. Let the demerits fall on his head! He will hold it up as long as he can.

All through that fall semester, from late August to the middle of December, I groped and stumbled in the alternate darkness and splendor of Dante. Scenes from the *Inferno* were the common ground I held with the fifty cadets who had elected my course. Together three mornings a week we looked at the famous dead in their infernal habitat, living eternally in some form of punishment. The cantos were our only bond, and together the students and I resisted or gave way to sympathy or antipathy as we read of Francesca and Thaïs, of Jason and Vanni Fucci. Scenes melted with scenes in that classroom, characters with characters. Those Dantean figures rose out of a fog of talk, and sank back again into more talk. The classroom became like another circle from which we could not escape, neither the jailed nor the jailer.

Every two Mondays I gave a "class paper," usually called a "ten-minute quiz," and I always announced I would be "at home" Sunday evening for any cadets who had questions on the cantos or who wanted to review the work done during the two weeks. Only a few came the first Sunday, but the number grew to an average of fifteen to twenty. A few students stayed on after the review session, and then from the questions they raised I could see what really interested them in Dante. The poem was one thing—that is what we concentrated on in class—but that poem provoked thoughts, raised questions about matters religious and moral that concerned them more deeply. They puzzled over the extremes of Christian thought: the optimism of St. Francis and the pessimism of St. Augustine. At one point when I was attempting to explain Manichaeism, one of the cadets who was grasping the problem blurted out—justifiably, I think—"How can anyone avoid Manichaeism? Isn't the world divided into two?"

In our informal conversation, after the formal review of Dante's text, the term that seemed strange to them, even new, and unusual even for the Catholic cadets, was the word "penitence." I imagine that "penitence" is used today even less than "sin." I tried to say that penitence is a joyous return to God. It is a blotting out of the unhappiness of sin.

I could count on a few of the cadets who easily wearied of talk about religion to turn the subject back to literature, especially to theories concerning the importance of literature, its weight, its power. With that turn, I was back on my own territory, from which I had seldom strayed throughout the years of my life. I had then to strive not to seem pompous, full of wisdom, arbitrary. How might I put big thoughts into simple speech? I wanted to appear honest to those young friends who were relaxed in my living room, and at the same time be truthful to myself.

I forget now the exact words I used, but my principal answer was something like: "Literature is our lasting proof of civilization." Then I tried to conjure up an example. We had been speaking in class of the *Vita Nuova* and the concept of courtly love. So I held out to those cadets this statement as an example of my claim: "Without literature we would have no real knowledge of the meaning of love. Literature is the richest memory we have of the universe."

They taxed me with the biggest questions, those cadets, and when they left me about ten or ten-thirty to go back to their barracks, I often plunged into feelings of shame over what I had said, shame over even attempting to answer their questions. One of them, Perry Patterson, from Spartanburg, a brilliant naturalist and deeply in love with literature, worried months in advance over which author to read intensively in an independent reading course. He wanted to choose Faulkner, and to choose him with equanimity he wanted me to say, "Faulkner is the greatest American writer." I never could quite say that, and Perry returned over and over again to the question, hounding me with it. Every time I told him, "Yes, read Faulkner for your course." But that was not enough. In the back of his mind was the thought that Virgil was the poet he should read, or Homer, or Sophocles. And in the back of my mind was the urgent thought I never expressed to Perry: "Read Proust or Joyce, or even Whitman."

Time, in its relentless passing, was the daily, hourly obsession with the cadets at VMI. This constant preoccupation made their lives different from the lives of students I had taught elsewhere. They could never relax into anything for very long: study, conversation, running, sleep. In fact, sleep often encroached on other activities: their presence in the classroom, their reading in the library, their attendance at mass. In each of those places, I have seen their heads bob and sink down—not through inattentiveness or disrespect, but simply through lack of sleep. Never in my life have I wanted to be a chairman or an administrator of any kind, except during my semester at VMI when I wished I might have the power to cut down on the cadets' time spent on parades and guard duty and exercise, and convert it into time for study and sleep.

During my first weeks in the classroom, as I watched my cadets march into the room and then sink down into their seats in a relaxed sitting position, legs stretched out ahead of them, I wondered if their remarkably straight-backed posture in marching was unnatural and forced. I soon realized, as I met them at other places on the post or in the town of Lexington, that their erect posture was natural. It had been acquired through training. With one exception, a sophomore, my cadets were juniors and seniors, and by then they were unable to walk otherwise. They had perfected a stance that demonstrated a physical power of the body, a virile alertness of control that had moved far beyond any conscious effort of exhibition. During afternoons the cadets seemed to be running everywhere and constantly, around the post, through parts of the town, and through the campus of Washington and Lee. I imagine the routes they followed, in good or bad weather, measured four or five miles. There, too, the form their bodies took in the running was admirable. Their litheness was natural. It reminded me of the swiftness I have seen in a running deer in the prehistoric cave drawings of Lascaux. Scenes from the film *Chariots of Fire* came to my mind, and Lexington turned into the site of a daily Olympic competition.

When, after a brief Christmas vacation in Durham, I returned to Lexington to teach for five months at Washington and Lee, I was already familiar with some parts of the campus, with the library and Evans dining hall, and a few of my future colleagues in the romance languages department.

The origins of the university go back to the middle of the eighteenth century, to Augusta College, founded by Scotch-Irish pioneers, twenty miles north of Lexington. In 1776, as a sign of patriotism, it was named "Liberty Hall." When it moved closer to Lexington in 1782, it was named "Liberty Hall Academy." George Washington saved the school in 1796 by an endowment gift, and in gratitude to the president it was named, first, "Washington Academy" and then "Washington College." Robert E. Lee became its president in 1865 for five years until his death in 1870. To honor his presidency, the name became officially "Washington and Lee University" because the School of Law had been added.

The Lee Chapel, constructed under President Lee's supervision, faces the Colonnade, a sequence of handsome columned buildings. Washington Hall in the center is flanked on one side by Newcomb and Payne, and on the other side by Robinson and Tucker. The remains of Lee are in the crypt of the chapel. At one time the cadets from VMI saluted whenever they passed in front of the chapel. It is no longer a rule they have to obey, but some still do this. I have seen it on a few occasions, this exemplary sign of respect. If you follow the same walk and pass the Lee Chapel, in the direction of Washington Street, you come to a small gray stone church, a parish church, the Robert E. Lee Episcopal Church. It is the only Anglican Church I know of named not after a canonized saint but a man—looked upon by many, of course, as a saintly figure.

One lives very close to history in Lexington. The two institutions, each of approximately 1,300 male students, preserve this history. They speak of it and celebrate it. At Washington and Lee the memory of General Lee is preserved especially in his chapel, and every president of the university is expected to be a worthy successor. At VMI the name of Stonewall Jackson, who once taught physics there, keeps returning. The cadets often reminded me that Stonewall Jackson was not liked by the cadets. They seemed to be warning me that if I expected to be liked by the cadets, I would have to behave differently from Jackson. Each day during the second semester, on my way home from the campus, I passed the Stonewall Jackson House, and knew that the tomb of Jackson was in the Lexington cemetery. In case of accident, I knew that the Stonewall Jackson Hospital was close to the Faculty Apartments on Estill Street.

Scheduled to teach two terms at Washington and Lee—the twelve weeks of the "winter term" (January through March) and the "spring term" of six weeks (April through May)—I began almost immediately to stand back from life as I viewed it on the campus, and even as I participated in it by means of the three classes I taught, along with my lunches at the Cockpit and evening meals at Evans dining hall. I knew I was on the margin of the life in this particular university, as it was being lived in the numerous fraternity houses scattered throughout the town and even surrounding my own apartment house, approximately a half mile from the center of the campus.

An undercurrent theme in conversations during my first months in Lexington concerned the absence of young women in the classes on the military post. There the possibility of a change, of the admission of women to VMI, seemed remote, almost impossible to imagine. (To myself I often said: it will come about, it is inevitable with the power today of the women's liberation movement.) Then beginning in January, with the slight geographical move, that theme grew to a sonorous one, resounding with strong accents of approval and disapproval. The majority of Washington and Lee students appeared to feel threatened by a feminine invasion. President Wilson was advocating this change, and some of his arguments seemed sound. A few students, articulate and vociferous, joined him. Could it be possible that such momentous change was to come in the immediate future?

The end of the first six weeks of the winter term was marked by a week's vacation in honor of Washington's birthday. By that time (February 1984), I knew that I would have to struggle to liberate my mind from the immediate parochial preoccupations of Washington and Lee (such as the admission of women and the wearing of ties to class), and the preoccupations of VMI. A few of the cadets continued to call on me when they were free to leave the post. Their topics were familiar: the undercurrent struggle between first-year class (seniors) and the administration concerning the "rat line," an indoctrination process administered by upperclassmen on freshmen.

It is too easy for me to become absorbed by the current preoccupations and gossip of an academic community, especially one that is new to me. I have always had to force myself to eliminate such matters from my mind when I return home from classes and meals with colleagues and students. I make that shift from the world of gossip to reality by reciting a sonnet of Mallarmé, by reading out loud a passage from Proust or a scene from *Phèdre*. Literature is for me a vast universality of memory. I have to resume a relationship with it whenever I feel myself being drawn into more temporary, more problematic matters. In social life, especially in unfamiliar social activities, I can feel on my face the forming of a mask, of an attitude that is forced and insincere. During my best moments of solitude I reach a state I might call guileless serenity. But in the most frenzied moments of an academic atmosphere, I live through the opposite state of mind.

In Lexington, Virginia, the days followed my pen. Those hours of time seemed there more precious than ever. I knew there that every absence from a friend is a prelude to the endless separation. The fragments I wrote there were mounds of reflection, to be inserted in some kind of narrative. André Gide once wrote that "our actions follow after us" (*nos actes nous suivent*), and I could easily add to that statement that our thoughts, too, follow us, our intentions and our imagination. These are weak formulas or phrases for what I am trying to say: no one escapes his destiny. The shadow of Oedipus falls over all of us. All the signs of our life which we heed so seldom are signs of our destiny. The weight of our past we tend to let shift from our conscious state into our subconscious.

Each day in Lexington I learned bits of history—traditional historical facts concerning George Marshall at VMI, Robert E. Lee at Washington and Lee, and Stonewall Jackson in the town itself. At the same time I learned local bits of history—gossip, really—concerned with the two institutions. I had to make a great effort to prevent these new lessons on history and tradition and gossip from taking over my conscious states and blotting out my lifelong interest in the arts and literature, in those problems of philosophy and theology that had sustained me throughout so many years.   .

The danger of any small restricted place—a small village or a small college, a fraternity or an academic department—is its exclusiveness, and the insidious subtlety by which it replaces the world. It is easy to encompass, and each member reasons with himself that he has no need to enlarge his horizon. Emerson used to say this about Concord, Massachusetts. But Emerson was a prodigious reader and a man of solitude. The world came into his life every day through his reading of Plato and Montaigne, when Concord turned into Athens and Bordeaux. Amherst, Massachusetts, was a similarly restricted site for the body of a woman whose mind remained active in its study of the self and all the enigmas of the self. Those brief poems of Emily Dickinson's are the same stage set where the poet's conscious self and unconscious self warred on one another.

My good friend Murray Vines, responsible for my being at Lexington, brought me every Monday his Sunday *New York Times*, leaving it on my porch at Letcher Avenue or at my apartment door at 2 Estill Street. By February I was accustomed to my new apartment, comfortable in it, and enjoying its novelty: the walk to school along Washington Street to the campus, and the return walk on Nelson Street, after picking up my mail from box 901. Those two walks formed a circle. Each crossed Main Street, and each allowed me to pass by several kinds of stores. Most of my practical needs could be met by purchases at those stores. I was constantly struck by the convenience of Lexington's layout: the barber shop was under the bank, the shoe repair shop was close to the bookstore and the cleaners. The three restaurants most used by students (and tourists), the two movie houses, and the post office were all placed strategically on Main Street and neighboring corners. On my daily walks I rehearsed them and the names of their streets. The walks gradually became too brief because store windows and buildings passed by so fast that I had little sense of exercise.

The Sunday *Times*, usually examined as part of Monday evening reading, opened up the world for me. During the weeks of February and March, I read first about two coming events which excited me and brought back rich memories, and then I read about them and their reception in New York. The first was the three-week season of the Martha Graham Dance Company, and the second was the retrospective show of Balthus, paintings that were leaving the Beaubourg in Paris for the Metropolitan Museum of Art in New York. The simple reading about these events in the early spring of 1984 brought back memories of Bennington in the late thirties, when I watched Martha Graham in the summers walking about the college campus with Louis Horst, and then watched her perform for the first time in public one of her dances: *Letter to the World*, for example. The name of Balthus brought back memories of Chicago in the late forties when I first heard his name from Jimmie Harrison and first studied some of his work in the Art Institute.

Thanks to the sympathetic writing of Anna Kisselgoff, I read about Graham's new dance of 1984, *Phaedra's Dream*, as I recalled the early version of *Phaedra* of 1962 which had centered on Phaedra's fatal lust for her stepson. Now in the new dance, Hippolytus is the center of interest in his dance with another male figure, the Stranger. For an entire month, *Phèdre* and the horses of Hippolytus seemed to fill my thoughts. I was teaching Proust in two classes where *Phèdre*, played by La Berma, returned often as a leitmotif for young Marcel. In the survey course I was teaching the Racine tragedy, scene by scene, and rehearsing with my students some of the great lines:

> Soleil, je te viens voir pour la dernière fois.

I was exiled in Lexington—it was a self-willed and even joyous exile—and the Greek legend of Phaedra and the ancient cult of Hippolytus I had read about in Gilbert Murray and other anthropological works were relating, in and out of the classroom, my present with my past. In the historical sense, the attacks made on Racine's tragedy when it was first performed—*la cabale de Phèdre*, as we call it in French classes—were not unlike the attacks made on Graham's first *Phaedra* which marked the beginning of her neoclassical art in the sixties. In *Phaedra*, as in the full-length *Clytemnestra*, Martha Graham used the dynamics of her modern dance technique to rehabilitate a primitive culture. With so many others, I too learned how to reexamine those primitive cultures in the ecstatic theater of Martha Graham, and once again, without being able in any satisfactory way to communicate this to my students in Virginia, I acknowledged to myself all I owe the American dancer who would be ninety in the spring of 1984. In my mind I could still see her on stage as Emily Dickinson (*Letter to the World*), as Emily Brontë (*Deaths and Entrances*), as Judith, as Hërodiade, as Phaedra. She has filled a part of my life more richly, more fully than any actress or any singer. In those scenes in Proust where Marcel speaks with Bergotte about the art of La Berma in *Phèdre*, the image of Graham on the New York stage gave substance to my words in the classroom.

Again, thanks to the *New York Times*, John Russell's article of February 19, 1984, told me of the Balthus show, on its way from the Pompidou Center in Paris to the Metropolitan Museum in New York. How accurate is Russell's term as he applies it to the paintings of Balthus: "their mesmerizing power." More than the subjects of the few paintings I have seen, I remember best their effect on me, their images that seemed to freeze me into a numbness. Their strange violence that Artaud spoke of in Paris at the time of the first one-man show, more than fifty years ago in 1934, he related to the violence of the age. A "diseased" era, Artaud called it. I am not sure that I understand that. I perhaps understand it in terms of Artaud's work more than I do in Balthus's paintings. He is the painter whose work I have read about more than I have looked at. (My exile in Lexington was all the more harsh because of this. Privileged New York!) There will be more articles on him now, beginning with Mark Stevens's fine essay in *Vanity Fair* (December 1983).

What is the source of Balthus's hallucinatory power, not unlike the power I have read in the books of his brother Pierre Klossowski? Is it the clarity of his sky? or the shadow across a girl's dress? or the strangeness of his young people in love? He is almost always erotic, but never vulgar. The few portraits I have seen are the subjects I like best, and in them I have tried to trace motifs of those painters from whose work he has drawn the most: Poussin, Piero della Francesca, Gustave Courbet. In Lexington, Virginia, I thought of Balthus, the Polish-French painter, during his years of exile away from Paris, and living today in Switzerland at the age of seventy-five as a confident, almost dogmatic man, containing within himself the superb force of a Byron. Deprived this year of seeing his painting *The Mountain*, or the drawings he did for *Wuthering Heights*, I who have reached his own age have to flog my flanks, but joyously, to continue with the life I have chosen.

As I imagined the heroic women I had seen Martha Graham dance —

Electra and Emily Brontë—and as I recalled in my mind the enigmatic young girls of Balthus, I rehearsed in Virginia, in this new setting of great beauty, all the problems of writing that have beset me through all the years of my life. In earlier years my goal had usually been to write a pioneer book, a critical book, about a French author who seemed important to me and who at that time had not been written about in English: Ernest Psichari, Maurice Scève, Rimbaud, Mallarmé. Today there are many studies about them by American and English scholars.

In these later years another set of problems besets me in the kind of writing I am attempting. Does journal-writing count as writing? Am I writing at too haphazard a gallop? Is this writing by its very nature too unquestioning, too unspeculative? Even a diary should aspire to some kind of form. The worst of writing is that one depends so much on praise. I try not to take praise or blame excessively to heart, but they interrupt my thoughts and the simple routines of each day.

If I find I am writing lugubriously, I have to remind myself that the only honest people are the artists, and not the reformers, not the statesman, not even the philanthropists. I have two ways of clearing my head: a little exercise in the air, and reading a few pages of good literature. In Lexington, if I wanted to learn how to write, I read every other day a few letters of Flaubert and a few entries in *A Writer's Diary* of Virginia Woolf. They helped me to know that even if my surface is agitated, my center is secure. They reminded me gently but firmly that there is no end to groping and experimenting.

After the celebrations in writing of Martha Graham and Balthus, a third subject began appearing in print everywhere. This time it was a subject that impinged directly on my course at Washington and Lee: the new film being made in France, and about to be released in Paris: *Un amour de Swann*. A French film, but cosmopolitan too, because its director was the German Volker Schlöndorff, already famous for his earlier film *The Tin Drum*. The character of Swann was to be played by Jeremy Irons, admired by all of us two years earlier in the television production of *Brideshead Revisited*. The part of Odette is played by Ornella Muti, an Italian actress whom I did not know but who was being acclaimed a great beauty.

By the time the first serious articles appeared, my students were well into the novel, past the first volume of *Swann's Way*, and well into the third volume, *Guermantes' Way*. We had spoken in class of the film about to be released, but the first information had been scanty. I had already told the class of the effort made several years earlier by Arthur Miller to write a scenario of "Swann in Love" for his wife Marilyn Monroe. She had wanted to play Odette. But the scenario, when it was finished, seemed inadequate to both Miller and Monroe. The project was abandoned, as it was to be abandoned by two other much stronger possibilities: Luchino Visconti in 1969, and Joseph Losey and Harold Pinter in the seventies.

I knew that the guiding figure behind these two projects to make a film that would embrace the entire narrative of *A la recherche* was Nicole Stéphane. From many years earlier I remembered her as a young actress in the part of Elisabeth in Cocteau's film, *Les Enfants Terribles*. The film had seemed to me good but not as strong or as dramatic as the novel. Edouard Dermit, destined to become the adopted son and heir of Cocteau, played the brother's role of Paul. The physical resemblance in the film of brother and sister, of Nicole Stéphane and Edouard Dermit, was a memorable triumph of the film. Throughout these last years Nicole Stéphane's name has always been associated with the film projects of Proust's novel. Finally in the spring of 1984, in Lexington, thanks to a copy of the new scenario sent to me from Paris by Ed Hamer, (the French professor I was replacing at Washington and Lee) I learned the reason.

Nicole Stéphane's mother was a friend of Proust's niece, Suzy Mante-Proust, the one heir of Proust who held all the rights to Proust's work. In 1962 this young actress had received permission from Mme Mante-Proust to make a film. Her first big hope for a director was Luchino Visconti, who had proved himself an admirable director of a film made from a story not unlike Proust: Thomas Mann's *Death in Venice*. The very subtle and beautiful camera shots of the arrival at the Hôtel des Bains on the Lido seemed to Nicole Stéphane a prefiguration of Marcel's arrival at the Grand Hôtel de Balbec.

When the Visconti project collapsed, Stéphane turned to the American director who had done most of his films in England: Joseph Losey. Two of Losey's films whose content seemed almost Proustian, *The Servant* and *The Accident*, have become cult films. When she approached Losey, he in turn approached the playwright Harold Pinter for a scenario that would comprise the entire novel. Pinter at that time had never read Proust. His first reading was a revelation to him, and he composed an elaborate scenario that has been published. The major film companies refused the Losey-Pinter project because it seemed to them too sumptuous, too ambitious, too expensive.

Peter Brook, the English director responsible for several important play productions in Paris, was interested in doing a film on Proust's novel. If films can be made from the novels of Balzac, Hugo, Stendhal, Zola, why not from

Proust's? The three French directors whom Nicole Stéphane considered approaching were usually authors of their own scenarios: François Truffaut, Alain Resnais, and Louis Malle. And Peter Brook was too preoccupied at the time by his production of *Carmen*. So she turned to Volker Schlöndorff, a longtime fervent reader of Proust and a skilled director, who, like Visconti, Losey, and Brook, has a sense of the spectacle, of an opera-theater.

Compromises were made on every side. Peter Brook and Jean-Claude Carrière worked on the text of the scenario by reducing the action of *Un amour de Swann* to twenty-four hours, with an epilogue which went to the death of Swann and which involves some scenes with the character of Swann's friend Charlus. Jean-Claude Carrière knew the planned adaptation of Pinter and Visconti. He and Peter Brook preferred to build the film around Charles Swann and follow him to his death. It is primarily a treatment of Swann at the highest moment of his passion for Odette, when he tirelessly made every effort to learn who Odette was, what her life had been.

When we read at Washington and Lee the scene of the Queen of Naples coming to the rescue of her cousin, le baron de Charlus, I told the class of Visconti's plan to have Greta Garbo play the Queen of Naples, Marlon Brando to play Charlus, and Jeanne Moreau to play Mme Verdurin. That was the plan in the sixties. In the seventies the Pinter-Losey production would have given great emphasis to "the little patch of yellow wall" (*le petit pan de mur jaune*) in Bergotte's death scene, and to the garden bell of Combray that announced visitors, and to Vinteuil's sonata for violin and piano.

But the film that was finally made concentrates on the sickness of love, on Swann's love for Odette, beginning with the night scene of Swann's frenzied search for Odette along the boulevards of Paris. In that scene of frantic agitation, Swann resembles Orpheus descending into the underworld to rescue Eurydice. In that scene and in the following scene of the *cattleyas*, he literally enters the hell of passion. The three leading characters in the film are all insular characters, overcome by their aloneness: Odette, a fatherless girl; Swann, a Jew in an anti-Semitic society; and Charlus, a homosexual pariah.

Graham, represented in her young company of dancers; Balthus, in his paintings exhibited in New York; and Proust, in the film finally made from *A la recherche*—these formed thoughts and references in my February and March classes at Washington and Lee. Many times I sensed that the world was there in the classroom, thanks to the recent history of dance and painting, of film and literature. When Graham spoke of the new dance she had devised for Hippolytus, she pointed out that a dream is a nightmare (night mare), the horse you ride at night. The hallucinatory power of the interiors of the Balthus paintings is similar to the power of Vermeer's interiors that Marcel Proust looked at in a Paris exhibition shortly before his death.

The word "estrangement" returned often to my conscious and unconscious mind during those late winter and early spring months in Lexington. Washington and Lee was a new world to face after I had become accustomed to the cadet world of VMI. What brought me back to reality was the two classes on Proust, thirty students in all, who gradually became familiar with Mélusine and the Faubourg Saint-Germain, with the avenue des Acacias and the name of Vinteuil. And thanks to those students, I too became familiar once again with those characters and places. During those hours when Balbec and Combray were more real for me than Lexington, my sense of estrangement diminished, and the great gloom that at times was in my mind disappeared. I was steadied by the passages in Proust which seemed to me the better part of my past, and steadied by my morning efforts to write some of these pages in my personal journal.

Estrangement is a fertile soil. There I can watch growing stronger than ever the minds, the literary minds I have loved the most fervently. There has been no drying up of those minds. The few *ballades* of Villon we read in the survey course, the *pensées* of Pascal, the opening of Rousseau's *Confessions*, these were clear sunlight streaming down over the rock to which I was chained. At times that rock was hard, the gadflies pungent, and the eagle's beak sharp to my liver.

And yet I continued stitching together the pages of a possible book. When in the spring term of six weeks I began reading with a large number of students, eighty in all, the *Inferno*, Dante replaced Proust for me and stayed with me constantly, not only in the classroom but in the early mornings when I continued to write out my thoughts about the past and about the present too, so clearly the offspring of the past. My life has often seemed to me a conflict between the words I utter in the classroom and the silent words I write in the morning notebook. I often catch myself confessing that I am too much in love with what I write. From such cogitations I often convince myself that I am out of fashion, and too old to teach. I am no longer interesting to the young. I am simply now obsolete.

15. A Letter to Myself About Rimbaud's Angel, with a Nod to Jim Morrison and His Doors

I can do no better than to list questions that move in and out of my mind as I write these pages. Are they simply messages to myself? Are they paragraphs of interest only to me? Are they a relaxed idiom not too far removed from the form of confessional poetry I have read in Roethke, in Plath, in Lowell?

I write about the self writing, and so persistently that my life has grown into a lost objectivity. I know all the terms that might be applied to these autobiographical probings: unbalance, compulsion, case history. A past self is company during the time when an incipient solipsism might declare itself and isolate me. A voice tells of the past and I take down the dictation in an effort to defy eccentricity and all discontents. Whenever I begin the act of writing, I feel that I enter boundless space and am working under the dark cope of sky.

I pursue this text—all these words and their punctuation—and it is thus I am able to breathe, it is thus that the text pursues me. The text is the ashes of a week that I have carefully swept into one corner of my lodging. Such an activity will then allow me to dream, to know both the experience of dreams and their reality.

In these pages I am calling a text, I am mirrored in syntax, suspended between two identities: a man who has a name and a man who has no name. I must have known very early in life that I had not inherited from my family and from my ancestors any sense of adventure. I would have to fabricate it, or rather conjure it up from the daily activity of reading, writing, teaching. *Un travail d'abeille*: a bee's slow, unremitting accumulation of a substance that comes from himself and from the chance clover he lights on.

A field of clover is a site too, not one that I distinguish clearly among the sites I have been recalling, because it has just now come into my mind as pure analogy. But the use of clover I have just made—an almost banal analogy—has brought back to my mind the vision and small of mimosa in Nice and along the roads leading into that city. Mardi Gras—a month or so before Easter—I have seen twice, when the city bedecked itself with the golden branches of that flower. It was a festive city then, feeling the rush of sap in the spring, and knowing the intercourse between heaven and earth, between sun and sea.

I would think then of other sites and seasons, of Vermont in autumn where I had seen partridges whirring up and birds in flocks appearing in gray, watery skies. One early morning in Pownal I watched a young friend break the back of a rabbit with a sharp knock of his hand, and I shuddered then at the generating of pain and death on that cold earth bearing no trace of broom or heather or mimosa.

My grandfather Adams was a gardener, who during the first years of my life lived in the same house with my grandmother and my Aunt Grace, but lived isolated from them, alone and taciturn, in a feud I never really understood. At the end of the day, when he returned home for supper, always consisting of two soft-boiled eggs, I would see clutched in his gnarled hands a bunch of roses from the gardens he tended, which he left on the kitchen table, and which, when he retired to his room, would be distributed among the women of the family, his wife and his four daughters, those very women who had ostracized him. As a child I thought of those flowers as tribute Grandpa Matthew Adams offered as a means to break the silence of that household and repair whatever injuries he had caused. Aunt Grace dutifully boiled the eggs for his supper, which he ate at the end of the kitchen table. His only companion was a large cat that rubbed its back against Grandpa's legs, and followed him up the stairs to his bedroom, into which he disappeared.

He lived in the gardens he tended, and in the kitchen and one bedroom of the house he had built practically with his own hands. He never once joined a family gathering. No one spoke to him except myself and Aunt Grace. As a young boy, I wondered about his plight, but never questioned anyone about it. Later, when I might have questioned and understood, too much time had gone by, and I felt it best to leave the mystery intact. Secretly I took my grandfather's side without knowing anything of the drama that must have occurred, probably before my birth. Secretly I decided as a boy that I would prefer to live alone rather than in a house, in the midst of a family where there might be silence and hostility.

A number of landscapes I have sketched on the pages of these books of memoirs or merely referred to: a Paris street, the Boston Public Gardens, the Duke campus and classroom 014, Central Park in New York, the small Giacometti park in Saint-Paul-de-Vence, a vineyard outside of Angers, the theater at Bennington College. Others I have not called upon because my memory of them is fainter: Gold Hill, two miles outside of Boulder, Colorado; Washburn Terrace in Brookline where I was born and rode a tricycle when I was three; Brooklyn College where I taught five classes one semester; the cathedral in Dresden where I heard mass in 1938 a few years before it was demolished by bombs.

Of all these varied sites, some drab and some exotic, classroom 014 is the most permanent picture in my mind. There I have had students almost uncouth, full of energy, with healthy bodies, but who seemed at the beginning of the semester beyond any possible relationship with the books I wanted to discuss with them. However, each one, as I gradually learned, possessed a curious and individual stability. That very stability of character helped me in trying to make the books kin to them. I have caught myself saying: "What you study here has been studied for five hundred years (Dante) or for fifty to sixty years (Proust). Let's hope that a heat will beat up over your consciousness."

After making some invisible connection with those students, I have felt dimmed by their departure. Even after a single class meeting that went well, I have felt a loss of myself, a lull in me, a passivity. But I knew then there would be other classes to come, and with that thought I would feel heavy impatience grip hold of me. I would be shaken out of my torpor.

From time to time there would be a blind, insistent figure standing over against me. It was hard for me, sometimes impossible, to find for him or her a new being, a new form. All would be well if I could succeed in leading the student into the art of Dante or into the thought of Proust. I was convinced that a new life could come out from such readings. (At another time in history, and in another place in geography, I would be sitting up with my ewes at lambing time. . . .) Classroom work is fragmentary and incomplete. But it can be the start of a voyage leading toward some greater ordering.

In those classes where I think in French and speak in French, I worry that I may appear to the students as some potent, cold, slightly hostile host. But the young have their own inscrutability, their own remoteness. Then suddenly there will be a coming together over a metaphor or a character. Those students: landscapes all of them. Each of those lives: a site too. Strangers in so many ways, and yet not strangers in other, more secret ways. For one like me, a foreign-language teacher, there will necessarily be foreignness between the students and myself. Florence and that world of the fourteenth century: Santa Maria del Fiore. Paris and that world of the twentieth century: Dreyfus and Réjane and Bergson and the Faubourg Saint-Germain.

As I teach this "foreignness," and try to make it into something universal and necessary for our American culture, I see in my mind, without referring to them in class, visions of those sites that have formed me. Saint-Paul-de-Vence: the end of the town turning into a cemetery, sweet that graveyard, perched on a hill catching the sunshine and far off from the constant glitter of the sea. Between the tombstones: the ubiquitous *fleurs de la Pentecôte* (that wild flower whose real name I have not yet discovered). The flowers glow like a presence among the trees. Beyond the tombs the heather comes rosy under the skies.

Nice, Saint-Paul, Saint-Jean-Cap-Ferrat—how far away from Brookline, from the snowstorms of my childhood that I still remember, and all the shoveling of snow from the seven steps leading up from the sidewalk to our porch. Have I, in middle age, in old age, lost my town, have I become someone else? Those early years appear gray and uniform now. I think of them from time to time when a burst of self-hurting fervor passes over me.

Spring for me now is North Carolina when berries shine red, when robins are seen, and when great droves of birds dash like spray overhead. In that season, more than in other parts of the year, I feel that secrets within the students are game for the teacher. It is then when they merge into some heavy obscurity. And I feel shame at playing the part of an easy blusterer. They have reason to glower at me and force a severance between them and me. At times in the spring my existence is annulled.

My life is a perpetual flux of perceptions. The course I teach for four months is like a birth, when I lose connection with a former self which also had lasted four months. There can come in that period of time a passionate exchange of thoughts, of wills, of minds. But when this does not come about, I have to learn to abate myself, to control myself, and to measure myself to the students.

My derivation from French is also my alienation.

My memory, as recorded in these three volumes, is the story of possibilities never totally fulfilled. I have sat safe and easy and unadventurous, with the unattainable always beyond me, with the subterranean force of desire always within me.

I have had students as aloof and shadowy as tigers. At first they are wild things wanting their distance. When they come to realize that I too am an alien, they approach me as a possible friend.

I have had students who were the centers of their universe, and who were unaware of anything outside. I continued to hope that they would come to realize I had an existence of my own. There were some who behaved with tolerant dignity. I remember others who carped and were loud over trifles. I enjoyed spying on those who exhibited a cavalier boisterousness.

The spoken word: how often in class it falls sterile on the unheeding students. Some do not want ideas and images dragged into consciousness. This I have felt most acutely in the course on the French Symbolists: in a close reading of a Mallarmé sonnet or a Rimbaud *illumination*. On those pages the metaphor has to be seen in some way or other, either the critic's way or the student's. There can be reluctance then to draw forth the image and see it clearly in some form of relationship, with the world itself, with the student's own background, and with the experience of the teacher. A Symbolist sonnet can be a life reconstructed: Nerval's *El desdichado*; or the image of a man's vocation: Mallarmé's *Pitre châtié*. Its very bigness and significance far outstrip its condensed form of fourteen lines. One hour's work on it in class suffices to reveal its power. When it succeeds in doing that, I have felt the deepest satisfaction a teacher can know. The opening lines of these sonnets are the microcosm of a man's life:

Je suis le ténébreux, le veuf, l'inconsolé (Nerval)

and of a man's vocation:

Yeux, lacs, avec ma simple ivresse de renaître Autre. . . . (Mallarmé)

Since the beginning of the eighties, because of an unusual encounter and an unusual investigation on my part, I have added to the lessons of Rimbaud a new one that has interested many of the young, my own students and those I have talked with in other colleges and high schools. In this way, Arthur Rimbaud has moved back into full focus for me, as I try once more to understand and teach the relevance and the beauty of his work. He is the poet who has attracted me during the longest period of time and on whose poems I have worked hardest in order to understand them and feel them myself, and then to help others enjoy them.

My Harvard professor, André Morize, barely touched on "Le Bateau ivre," but I listened one day to an explication of the poem at Wellesley College, given by Marguerite Mespoulet. Gertrude, the girl I was visiting at Wellesley, was as proud of her professor as I was of mine. When she spoke of Rimbaud,

Mlle Mespoulet far outshone Morize. She was an erratic, brilliant teacher, the first I imagine in this country to speak of Max Jacob, and one of the first to have a deep feeling for the beauty and power of Paul Claudel. One day at Wellesley I heard her end a class with a question to which she gave an immediate answer —and then rushed out of the classroom:

> "Qui est Paul Claudel?"
> "Claudel, c'est l'Espagne."

Fifty-five years have gone by since Mespoulet shouted that sentence which I am still trying to understand. She was the first to reveal to me Rimbaud as a poet of flight, as a poet of many sites. Since that time I have often confused the sites in the life and work of Rimbaud with those places in which I have lived, within and without my own country. A curious identification has been established, thanks to geographical hyperbole.

One of the oldest publishing houses in Paris, Le Mercure de France, brought out several years ago, long before the Pléiade and other editions, a volume called *The Complete Works of Rimbaud*. It was far from complete, but it was a handsome book, on excellent paper, with good printing, and containing a preface by Paul Claudel that was destined to become famous and controversial. Through the years this edition was kept in print and always inexpensively priced. When the cost of books went up considerably, this first edition that called itself *oeuvre complète* retained its original price. I used it when I first began teaching Rimbaud in Vermont, and my students were appreciative of the book's appearance and its price.

A few years ago I had to call at Le Mercure de France on a very minor business matter. Unexpectedly I found myself being ushered into the office of the director. I apologized for troubling him, but since I was there, and since M. Hartmann appeared very cordial, I told him how curious I had been about his edition of Rimbaud, and asked him how he had been able to keep the price so low for so many years. I remember he smiled then and said, "Since you have come from quite a distance, I'll let you in on a house secret. We have been living on that book for several years."

I was frankly puzzled, and asked him what he meant. He replied, "Let me put it in figures. For the past twenty years we have been selling the Rimbaud volume on an average of thirty-two copies a day. This includes, of course, sales throughout the world, in South America, for example, where French books have a good market." And then M. Hartmann drew a conclusion—and this is the reason for my telling the story. He believed that every day, somewhere in the world, a few young people are discovering the poems of Rimbaud and are eager to own their personal copy of the book.

I agreed with him, and today, with more recent statistics I have been able to collect, I would guess that Rimbaud is the most widely sold modern poet. The rock music world paid considerable attention to Rimbaud in the sixties and seventies. The popular singers of the sixties, and the numerous critics who have written about Rimbaud since then, and the huge bibliography on Rimbaud collected by Étiemble for his thesis, *Le mythe de Rimbaud* (40,000 items from every possible country)—all this is ample proof that it is difficult to approach Rimbaud with impartiality. Either his work appears too difficult on first reading and is dropped by the lazy reader, or the attraction to this young rebel is so strong that readers of every age tend to praise him in excessive terms. In the heyday of surrealism, André Breton called him "the god of adolescence." A few years later, in wartime, Albert Camus called him "the greatest poet of revolt."

During his relatively brief life (1854–91), Arthur Rimbaud moved about considerably in a geographical sense. His first escapes were vagabond flights that did not go far from his home in Charleville (northern France): to Paris, to Belgium, and to London. These were the four or five years, between the ages of sixteen and twenty, when he produced the whole of his literary work.

After he stopped writing poetry, about the age of twenty-one, his life itself became an epic and he literally lived the voyages he had written about as voyages of his mind and his imagination. Between 1874 and 1880 his life was spent in a series of attempted flights: London, Stuttgart, Milano, Sienna, Java, and back to Charleville. This was the end of what some critics have called his period of vagrancy, his period of wandering about, largely in Europe. His brilliant precocity was followed by a sudden renunciation of literature: the source of many conjectures and legends which every student of Rimbaud has tried to solve.

Between 1880 and 1890 Rimbaud lived and worked for a business firm in Aden, on the southern tip of Arabia, and in inland Ethiopia, and then, on his own account, as a trader in the deserts of Abyssinia. The hundred or so letters Rimbaud wrote during those last eleven years of his life to his mother and sister in Charleville reveal a need to journey into the unknown, not as a poet but as a trader equipped with a treatise on artesian wells, for example. The early writing done in Europe, poems and letters on poetic theory, and the letters written during the last years of his life in Africa and Asia reveal a similar aspiration for knowledge and power, and a similar acceptance of the state of solitude. By different means Rimbaud expressed the same thought in one of his greatest poems, "Les poètes de sept ans," and in a letter from Aden in 1882, when he writes: "The main thing, and the most urgent for me is to be independent, no matter where."

The last year of his life, 1891, was a period of intense physical suffering from a tumor on his right knee. He made an agonizing return to France, to Marseille, where in the Hospital of The Immaculate Conception his leg was amputated. He died in that hospital in November and was buried in Charleville, where today his grave is visited by many of his readers.

The poems of Rimbaud and his letters represent a quest for self-fulfillment. It was pursued to such extremes, both in the writing and in the hazardous risks he knew on continents other than Europe, that today the flight has taken on the power and the prestige of a symbol. It may well be the central motif in his poetry around which all the others gravitate.

One of his early escapes from home was to Charleroi and Belgium. In the sonnet "Ma Bohème" he is Orpheus in the Ardennes where, seated on the side of the road, he rhymes and plucks the laces of his wounded shoes as if they were the strings of a lyre, one foot near his heart. I have often thought this scene not unlike the picture of a hippie guitarist.

Between October 1870, probable date of "Ma Bohème," and his trip to Paris in September 1871, when he met Paul Verlaine and when his life changed considerably, Rimbaud wrote the sonnet "Oraison du soir," in which he is more provocative, more bent on shocking his readers. Seated at a café table, the poet says: "I live seated like an angel in the hands of a barber":

Je vis assis tel qu'un ange aux mains d'un barbier.

Traditionally a large white cloth covers a man seated in a barber shop, and traditionally an angel is painted, or imagined, wearing a white robe.

These opening words (I believe it is Rimbaud's first use of the word *ange*) are almost a declaration of an adolescent of sixteen scorning a life of action. The drinker is the dreamer, and the dreams are so numerous that the glasses of beer too are numerous. The poet says he drank thirty to forty mugs of beer and then had to go outside to relieve himself with the consent of the tall heliotropes in the garden.

The last tercet of the sonnet opens with a solemn biblical line: "the Lord of the cedars and the hyssops." The Lord is evoked (the poem is called "Evening Prayer") at the moment of urination. It is a scene that will return in Joyce's *Ulysses* where Stephen Dedalus and Leopold Bloom urinate in the garden of Bloom's house after drinking several cups of tea. Heliotrope is a hieratic flower that honors the sun by turning toward it—the Sun that might be looked upon as the Lord of all plants.

> Doux comme le Seigneur du cèdre et des hysopes,
> Je pisse vers les cieux bruns, très haut et très loin
> Avec l'assentiment des grands héliotropes.

In the last section of "Une saison en enfer," Rimbaud calls himself by two titles, or two names: *mage et ange*. *Magus* in the literal sense of priest (or magician), and *angel* in the Rimbaud sense of a man relieved of morality. This sense of "angel" appealed to the rock singers of the sixties ("flower children," "flower power") who saw in Rimbaud a man purified of the world's corruption. This is one clue to the power of Rimbaud today, to the continuing influence he exerts on young people and young poets. Bob Dylan speaks of Rimbaud in his songs, recommends him and exalts him.

This is a phenomenon, difficult to analyze, but one that will have to be assessed and explored in any study of spirituality in today's world. In the film *Teorema*, Pier Paolo Pasolini, without mentioning the name of Rimbaud, quotes lines from the poems and especially the prose poem, "Déserts de l'amour." In another film, *Help!* the second film by the Beatles, there is an outside mountain snow scene, featuring a grand piano, surrounded by the four Beatles. It is unmistakably drawn from Rimbaud's prose poem "Après le déluge," with the line:

> "Mme X establishes a piano in the Alps"

If you listen carefully (the sound track is low-pitched), you will hear Ringo, who is seated at the piano, recite, with an almost unrecognizable French accent:

> Mme X établit un piano dans les Alpes.

I believe it would be possible for young readers today to sense the art of Rimbaud, his drives, his ambitions, and his accomplishments during the very few years when he wrote poetry, if it were done in terms of the rock singer (still popular with high school and college students) Jim Morrison. He was the controversial singer and lyricist of the group called The Doors, first heard in 1967, who mysteriously died in Paris, in July 1971. Four years of performances, before which and during which he constantly read Rimbaud, according to his biographers in their book: *No One Here Gets Out Alive*. The parallels between the lives of the French poet and the American singer-poet are striking: the absence of a father and the presence of a strong-willed mother, attitudes of rebellion, the seriousness about rebellion, the themes of violence and pathos in the poems of Rimbaud and in such songs of Morrison's as "Light My Fire," "Touch Me," and "Riders on the Storm." Even if the biographers Jerry Hopkins and Daniel Sugerman had not told us about Morrison's study of Rimbaud, I would have guessed it.

In 1966 I published my translation of Rimbaud's *Complete Works*. It was, I believe, the first published translation in a bilingual edition. It has been kept in print ever since. During the following three or four years I received a few notes, from persons I did not know. They were brief thank-you notes, sent to the publisher, for my having done the translation. One of those notes was from Jim Morrison, who wrote: "Just wanted to say thanks for doing the Rimbaud translation. I needed it because I don't read French that easily. Rimbaud means a great deal to me." At the bottom of the page were the words: "I am a rock singer."

I confess that at the time I did not know who Jim Morrison was. But I kept his letter with the others that came in. Not until 1980, nine years after his death, did I listen to the albums of The Doors.

Shortly before his death in 1971 Morrison visited the cemetery of Père LaChaise in Montmartre in order to see the graves of Edith Piaf, Balzac, Chopin, Gertrude Stein, Proust, and Modigliani. A few days later he was buried there, and today forty to fifty youths each day, from England and America and other countries, troop there to pay tribute to Jim Morrison. They drink beer at the grave, smoke marijuana, and write graffiti messages on the tomb and on surrounding tombs. A map is not needed to find the grave. There are helpful arrows pointing in the right direction, with the words: "Jim straight ahead." Smaller groups of young people visit Rimbaud's grave in Charleville. I have visited both graves, Rimbaud's in the fifties and Morrison's on my last visit to Paris in 1980, when I deciphered among the graffiti a line of my translation of the sonnet "Oraison du soir": "I piss toward the dark skies, very high and very far, with the consent of the large heliotropes." A strong line, I thought, that Jim himself might have chosen.

These are the two names—Rimbaud and Morrison—which during the past five years have filled my conscience and consciousness with the word *sites*. The sites in the lives of the poet and the singer are far more dramatic and more significant than the sites in my own commonplace life of a French teacher. The Rimbaud sites: Charleville, Paris, Brussels, Stuttgart, Aden, Marseille; and the Morrison sites: Los Angeles, New York, Madison Square Garden, Mexico,

Paris, Père LaChaise,—have guided me in the rehearsal of the sites I have wanted to celebrate in this book.

The word most closely related to this book's title is *doors*. I was at first puzzled by the choice of this word designating the rock group of four fellows: Ray, the pianist-organist; John, the drummer; Robby, the guitarist; Jim, the tenor-baritone singer and poet. Why The Doors? But I know now that the phrase comes from William Blake: "If the doors of perception were cleansed, everything would appear to man as it truly is, infinite." Aldous Huxley took it as the title for his book: *The Doors of Perception*. And Jim Morrison named his band *The Doors, open and closed*. During this search for my own past, I have followed, often subconsciously, the examples of these two Dionysian spirits of France and America who dared not only to open doors but also to close them.

In order to enter the City of Dis (*Inferno*, canto 9), Dante and Virgil needed the help of an angel who with the touch of his wand opens the gate. And Homer, centuries before Dante, speaks in the *Odyssey* (XIX, 560–65) of two gates: the ivory gate opening onto sites of fantasies and dreams of illusions, and the gate of horn, more honest, more realistic in what it offers to mortals. Gates of risk and adventure, as well as gates of portentous truths.

Index

Library of Congress Cataloging-in-Publication Data
Fowlie, Wallace, 1908–
Sites : a third memoir.
Includes index.
1. Fowlie, Wallace, 1908–   . 2. French literature—
Study and teaching (Higher)—United States. 3. Critics—
United States—Biography. 4. College teachers—United
States—Biography. I. Title.
PO67.F65A36   1986   840'.9   [B]   86-19760
ISBN 0-8223-0700-6